Never go hungry!

Jacques · 2019

How to cook
100% Vegan

Hungry Soul

The Hungry Soul Series

Vol. 1

Jacques Brennan

Matador
9 Priory Business Park,
Wistow Road, Kibworth Beauchamp,
Leicestershire, LE8 0RX
Tel: 0116 279 2299
Email: books@troubador.co.uk
Web: www.troubador.co.uk/matador
Twitter: @matadorbooks

ISBN 978 1789015 461

British Library Cataloguing in Publication Data.
A catalogue record for this book is available from the British Library.

Printed and bound by CPI Group (UK) Ltd, Croydon, CR0 4YY
Typeset in 10pt Minion Pro by Troubador Publishing Ltd, Leicester, UK

Matador is an imprint of Troubador Publishing Ltd

For Carmel, Isabelle, Thomas, Emma, Colm and Anne-Marie – who never hesitated to comment, praise or criticise when necessary.

For all who sat at my table and endured my many gastronomic attempts and concoctions.

No part of this book may be torn out or damaged in frustration.

Splatters arising from the liberal use of olive oil and/or staining from
tomato sauce will be tolerated and are
not considered as defacement.

We* cannot be held responsible for any
unsuccessful cooking creation.

Cooking is an art and not a science; come to think of it, science is not
perfect and in fact, to err is human… sorry, I get carried away,
I think you get the idea.

All masterpieces come with time, after much practice, many attempts
and an element of luck. What we can guarantee is that, if you follow what
we have tried to convey here,
you will not go hungry!

*The collective souls who have
helped shape this opus.*

MAKE THIS.
3 MINUTES . . . Y*ummm!*

"I can't believe it's as simple as tomatoes, garlic and olive oil."

*Emma, a daughter's reaction upon
tasting my bruschetta.*

TOMATO BRUSCHETTA

Contents

ESSENTIAL FARE

MEALS

APPENDIX

The Inside Story?

... from the author's mouth.

It all started in the kitchen…

I watched my mother cook. Her French style – simple dishes, many salads, plenty of fresh herbs and never less than five or six parts to the meal.

As soon as I was old enough, I was 'asked' to help. Cooking for seven was a lot of work: peeling carrots, peeling potatoes, washing lettuce and washing dishes! I learnt to make soup, to cook rice, to boil pasta, to toss the salad and to make home fried potatoes – my father's contribution. My mother had her own way of doing things and we were taught to follow them: vegetables chopped small and uniformly, very little salt and parsley on everything. Before leaving home, we children all knew how to cook and, I might add, quite well… my opinion!

As I got older and more independent, I wanted things my way and this was no different with cooking. I development my own style… garlic on everything, lots of chilli and pools of olive oil. I might come home from college and cook a nice chilli. Turning my back, my mother would be adding something to my dish… tampering with my cooking! Two cooks in one kitchen is a recipe for disaster.

Today, those who cook in close proximity are often subjected to a comment or two or, even worse, a slight doctoring of their dishes. I have been known, when invited to someone's home for dinner, to enter their kitchen and taste the meal. If I consider it necessary and the cook is not looking, I might add a little more salt, a little seasoning or perhaps an extra drop of olive oil…

My first attempts at writing a cookbook came when my wife's younger brother visited us for several days. When leaving he asked if I could write down a few recipes of the food he had been enjoying. I put together a little opus for him, one which I found recently, oil stained, tomato splattered, but still in use more than 20 years later.

Not so long ago, as my children left home for college, I started to receive requests for recipes – they missed their father's cooking! Upon reflection I realised that they were likely not the only ones in need of culinary direction – many young adults are leaving home without the necessary skilled to feed themselves.

After much rumination, I put pen to paper, fingers to the keyboard and the seeds to *Hungry Soul* were planted. I felt compelled and obliged to impart some of this accumulated cornucopia of knowledge to the many hungry souls out there… I hope it helps.

Jacques

COOKING

If you have never done much cooking, it may seem a little daunting at first. All you need is to start. You will make mistakes. The food will not be as expected, but do not panic. With time and hunger, you will soon master this important and very easy skill.

A Few Rules

... not to be broken.

Before you start cooking, read these and follow them.

... highly recommended!

1. **Read through the recipe!** – I have been halfway through making a dish only to realise I have left out something important... too late! Read the complete recipe before you start cooking.

2. **Use your hands** – There are no better tools – just wash them well. Great when mixing, tossing salad, anything. (Do not use plastic gloves... you just don't know where they have been!)

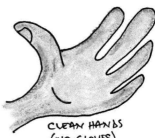

CLEAN HANDS
(NO GLOVES)

3. **Use sharp knives** – The most important tool in your kitchen. Have a good big one and keep it sharp; see the Appendix for sharpening.

4. **Taste it** – Ingredient use may vary. Some days one is heavier-handed with the salt, at other times the oil. Taste as you cook to be sure you are doing the right thing, then adjust it to your liking.

5. **Improvise** – All set to cook, but you do not have all the ingredients, no worries. Look at your shelves, open the fridge, take stock. Most recipes can be varied with different vegetables, beans, etc. Or make something else!

6. **Keep trying** – When you start cooking you will be hesitant, things may not turn out as expected. Just start again, it is the only way.

7. **Tidy as you cook** – Finished with an ingredient? Put it away. It helps keep your cooking area clear. Wash the mixing bowl, the knife, the spoon, while things are cooking. You will have less to do at the end. After the meal I am definitely not in the mood for cleaning up!

You Are What You Eat

... so eat the best.

Be your best, eat the best. Your body functions on what you put into it. The better food you eat or drink, the better it will run; common sense, so follow it.

Good Food Types

When we eat plant food, we are eating food directly from the energy and nutrient sources – the earth and sun.

Grains	= starches	= energy source
Beans	= proteins	= muscle building
Nuts	= fats	= body function
Veggies	= vitamins	= brain power

... I eat a lot of veggies!

"This unscientific analysis may be a little simplified, but the general idea is good. You need some of each for that perfect body and mind!"

Quality Food

Whole Food

Unrefined – white often means the goodness has been removed. Look for complete food, i.e. brown rice, wholegrain breads.

Organic Food

Plants grown without the use of chemical fertilisers or pesticide – 100% natural.

Home-Cooked Food

When you cook yourself, it is fresh and you know exactly what goes into your meal. No nasty preservatives, excessive salt or sugar.

Mood Food

... comfort food.

What you eat stimulates the body – positively or negatively – and affects the mind, the mood – the whole system is connected.

Good Food = Good Mood

Comfort Food

Know your comfort food. Mine is warm boiled potatoes with chopped fresh garlic, a little salt and drizzle of olive oil... Happy!

Water

When I am tired I drink 500ml of water all at once. I feel it trickle down inside me and almost immediately feel better, revitalised.

Green leaf salad

Green leaf salads are light, fresh, and easy to digest. Tired, need to eat something? Eat salad.

Power soup – green soup

Pure power. Green Soup (Soupe Verte). When sick yet hungry, this is all you should eat – one good bowl will have you jumping out of bed.

Short Grain Brown Rice

Organic short grain brown rice is a special food. When I eat short grain brown rice I feel better. Complete, slow energy release food… no tiring blood sugar rush.

Fasting, eating less

Fasting is just refraining from eating for a period of time. The energy saved from not having to digest is used by the body to heal and repair itself. Give the body a rest.

Upset stomach? Do not put more into it, give it a break.

Tools

... utensils.

To cook you will need a few tools. You do not need many but buy good quality utensils. They are more expensive, but they will last longer and, more importantly, they will work much better.

You may choose to gather all these together or you can slowly collect them, buying as the need arises. Better yet, have one of your wonderful parents or guardian angels make you a gift of them as you leave the house.

Chopping board
Box grater
Knives
Oven tray
Frying pan
Vegetable peeler
Potato masher
Pots
Wooden spoons
Tea towels
Large mixing bowl
Colander
Spatula
Blender

Chopping board – When choosing a chopping board, bigger is better; veggies don't keep falling off, great as a hot pot holder and it can hold an entire large pizza!

Wooden boards are the best. Wood is easy on the knives, it has natural antiseptic properties and is nice to look at.

Colander – A large bowl with holes, a strainer, made from metal or plastic. Use it for draining pasta, washing vegetables, grains, and beans.

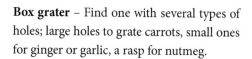

Box grater – Find one with several types of holes; large holes to grate carrots, small ones for ginger or garlic, a rasp for nutmeg.

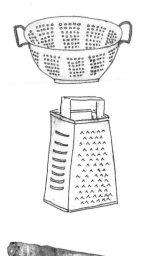

Knives – A big knife is essential. The blade should be at least twice as long as the handle. This will be the most important tool in your kitchen. A small paring knife will come in handy for fruit or peeling veggies. Keep them sharp.

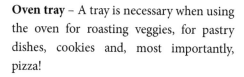

Oven tray – A tray is necessary when using the oven for roasting veggies, for pastry dishes, cookies and, most importantly, pizza!

Frying pan – To start with get a large heavy frying pan, the non-stick type makes your life easier – and easy to clean. 30cm/12 diameter is a good starting size.

Vegetable peeler – Used for peeling carrots, parsnips, turnips, potatoes and fruit.

Potato masher – Have a strong one with a flat head. The flat head enables you to make smooth textures. Apart from using it to mash spuds, I also use it to reduce chunky soups to a chowder and to make tomato sauce. Once the veggies are cooked, mash them up.

Pots – You should have a large pot (3 litres) and a small one (1 litre). The large one will be used to make soup, boil water for pasta, cook potatoes, nearly everything. A small pot is great for sauces and reheating small quantities of leftovers.

Wooden spoons – Have several on hand; when cooking you are often making more than one dish. Long-handled wooden spoons are perfect and gentle on that non-stick pan.

Tea towel – A multi-purpose piece of cloth that is used to dry dishes. Also, a hot pot holder, an oven mitt, you can even use it to dry lettuce and even for wiping your hands. Have two or three.

Large mixing bowl – A large bowl you will use every day. It can be used for pizza dough, making burgers, anything that needs mixing. I find the light stainless-steel ones the best.

Spatula – A long-handled implement with a flat blade used to flip food such as pancakes, burgers, cookies or croquettes.

And if the purse strings allow it...

A Blender – A hand blender or plunge blender was once popular and cheap, but today the **'bullet blenders'** are common – a traditional blender turned upside down.

They are designed for making smoothies, but I use it for sauces, soups, making breadcrumbs, herbs – anything I want to reduce; a great invention.

The Pantry

... your special stash.

On a shelf or in your cupboard keep a few ingredients that you will use every day such as salt & pepper, olive oil and garlic… no kitchen should be without them.

I keep a few more – spices and herbs are really a must for your chilli and curry or soup.

Fresh garlic
Whole black pepper
Extra virgin olive oil
Vegetable oil
A few dried herbs & spices
Dijon mustard
Sea salt
Tinned tomatoes
Apple cider vinegar
Nutritional yeast

Fresh Garlic – One of nature's very special ingredients.

Apart from its life-giving healing properties, it gives dishes a wonderful flavour. Once you get the appetite for it, you will want to use it in nearly everything; it is addictive. I have lots on hand.

Whole Black Pepper – Black pepper gives a spicy taste without the heat that comes from chilli. Used on top of pizza, with tomato sauce, with creamy dishes, a must sprinkled over oven chips. Use a pepper mill so you have fresh ground pepper each time.

Olive Oil (Extra Virgin) – 'Extra virgin' means mechanically pressed, not extracted by chemical means as with many commercial oils. If it is cold pressed it is even better. It just tastes great. I use it instead of butter in all dishes, even in cakes! Olive oil is not recommended for frying as at high heat it develops nasty elements – perfect for salad dressing or drizzling over any food.

Vegetable Oil – Vegetable oil is good for frying and cooking, use grape seed, rape seed/canola oil, or sunflower oil. Mechanically pressed highly recommended, cold pressed is best and if organic even better.

Sea Salt – Salt from the sea has a special taste and minerals which are good for you – extra benefits at no extra cost!

Apple Cider Vinegar – You will need vinegar to make salad dressing or vinaigrette. Use apple cider vinegar. It has many other important benefits, especially as a natural kitchen first aid kit – it relieves pain when applied to skin burns!

Dijon Mustard – Mustard is an emulsifier; it helps to keep the oil and the vinegar together when making vinaigrette or mayo and in creamy sauces. Of course, it adds a lovely taste. Use Dijon. It is great with home fries!

Tinned Tomatoes – I use tomato in so many dishes that I always have tins on the shelf. They are used to make tomato soup, for pizza sauce, for pasta sauce, in curries, in dahl, in chilli, refried beans, and with chickpeas – never be without them!

Nutritional Yeast – This is a neutralised yeast, no longer active. It gives a full and nutty flavour to food apart from important nutrients. I use it to give the umami (savoury) flavour to food: in mashed potato, in cream sauces or added to most savoury dishes.

N.B. Get the fortified type with added B12, a most important vitamin that is sometimes difficult to get from other foods.

Herbs & spices

Herbs and spices give flavour. Fresh herbs give food life.

Spices:

Mild curry powder – for Indian dishes.
Chilli powder – for chilli.
Dried chilli flakes – to spice things up!
Cumin seeds – for stews, chilli and in Indian dishes.
Black pepper – to flavour soups, potatoes and sauces.

SPICES

Dried herbs:

Oregano (dried) – good for all cooked tomato dishes.
Thyme (fresh or dried) – used in soups, sauces and stews.
Bay leaf; for soups and stews.

OREGANO DRIED

Fresh Herbs:

Coriander (cilantro) – for tomatoes, salads, Indian food.
Basil – used on fresh tomatoes, with pasta and in salads.
Parsley – great in soups, salads, with mushrooms or garlic bread.

PARSLEY

FRESH HERBS

How To Cook

... creative work!

To me, cooking is pure pleasure. Actually, it is creativity and what you produce is art. The best part – you get to sample your work. And you get to do it over and over again.

Preparing

... get ready.

Preparing or 'prepping' – term used in the culinary industry for preparing food.

You have taken out the necessary ingredients for your dish and a little preparation is required.

Vegetables

Vegetables sometimes need to be trimmed of wilted edges, or removing the outer protective layers. For many a quick rinse under the tap will suffice.

Asparagus – Take the length in two hands and snap off the bottom bit, approx. 4cm/2 inches or less – this is a woody section you want to discard. Rinse and cook the upper part.

Avocado – Make sure the avocado is ripe. Press it a bit with your thumb; if it gives, it is ripe. Cut the ripe avocado in two lengthwise around the stone, remove the stone from the middle and then peel the rest or scoop out the flesh from the thick skin.

Carrots/parsnips – Carrots and parsnips are usually peeled, but if young, fresh and organic, just wash.

Cauliflower – Discard the green outer leaves. Trim any browned or discoloured parts on top, then rinse.

Chilli pepper – Rinse them and cut off the top stem. The seeds are hotter than the flesh, so if you fear they might be too hot, discard them before chopping up the rest.

Fresh herbs – A quick rinse, then dry with your tea towel. Cut away the thicker stems and mince the leaves to desired size with your big knife. With basil, I just tear the leaves with my hands.

Garlic – Remove the outer dry skin. Cut off the bottom hard bit of the clove, then with the side of your large knife press down on the clove which cracks the skin and it easily comes off.

Green beans – Rinse under running water and trim the top and bottom ends.

Lettuce – Wash in a bowl of water. Drain off the water then place the leaves on your clean tea towel. Gather up the corners and give it a good few spins – better done outside!
(If you have a salad spinner you do not need the tea towel.)

Leeks – The long leeks look very clean, but inside the layers can hide fine sand. Slice them in two lengthwise and rinse well between the layers under running water.

Onions – Remove the outer dry layers by cutting the onion in two along the length then trim the top and bottom.

Potatoes – Wash well. They can be cooked with their skins which adds taste and nutrients! But you can also peel the skin before cooking them.

Spinach – Wash well. If the leaves are large, cut out the thick stems and tear the leaves into smaller pieces.

Sweet peppers – Rinse them, remove the stem part as well as the seeds and any white pith.

Tomatoes – Rinse, cut in two and remove the stem and the light coloured firm core.

Fruit

All fruit have seeds or stones in them; the small ones can be eaten, the bigger ones need to be removed and discarded.

Apples/pears – Cut them in two and remove the seedy core. You can peel them or not depending on the texture you want to create.

Cooking apples – Normally these have thick skins that are better peeled.

Bananas – Remove the skin before consuming.
Careful where you discard it, they are known to be very slippery underfoot!

Berries – Rinse gently under running water, pat dry and eat.

Plums – Wash them, split in two and remove the centre stone.

Pineapple – Peel it. You may also need to trim off small hard points which remain. The centre core is quite hard and fibrous, cut it out as well.

Oranges – Remove the outer skin before using the flesh, or cut in two and squeeze out the juice. If using the rind (outer skin), wash them well first.

Lemon/limes – For juice, cut them in two and squeeze. You may need to use the rind (outer skin) – wash well, then grate the skin using the smallest of holes on your grater – for this, try and buy them unwaxed.

Mango – The stone is quite big and is almost the width of the fruit. Cut away each side of it and use the flesh.

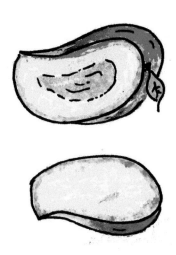

Beans & Lentils

Beans and lentils are sold dried in packages. Rinse well to remove any dirt or dust.

Kidney/pinto beans & chickpeas – These can take a long time to cook, so a period of soaking reduces the cooking time and once re-hydrated they are less likely to break apart in cooking.

Soaking for a few hours, even overnight, is recommended.

Black beans – Black beans do not take as long to cook as kidney beans or chickpeas, but a few hours soaking does shorten the cooking time.

Lentils – Lentils cook quite easily; no soaking is required, they can be put into the pot once rinsed.

Grains

Grains are full of starch and this can accumulate in the bag they come in. Rinse well before cooking otherwise it may turn out stickier then desired.

Rice – Rinse well before adding to the pot.

Millet – Rinse well before adding to the pot.

Quinoa – The seeds have an outer bitter casing. Soaking for a half hour helps reduce some of it. Discard the water before adding to the pot.

Chopping It Up

... cutting down to size.

Chopping can be art in itself. Actually, it is part of the preparation process, but since it is a crucial part, I made a separate section.

> *NOTE: Make sure the knife is sharp. I sharpen mine almost every day. See Appendix for instruction.*

Chop – Cutting into pieces. Generally, the recipe will indicate the sizes or the shape required, i.e. finely, coarsely, into large chunks, etc…

Cube – Cutting into squares of more or less equal size – 1cm/½ inch.

Dice – Chopping into small cubes of equal sizes about 5mm/¼ inch in dimension.

Grate – Using a grater, you reduce the item to small strips in various sizes depending on the holes available on your grater.

Julienne – Cutting into very fine strips; can be for peppers or celery, carrots… used for stir fries or salads.

Mince – Cutting into very small pieces so that the item becomes well blended in the dish, such as with garlic, ginger or fresh herbs.

Rounds – Cutting cylindrical vegetables such as cucumbers, carrots, parsnips, aubergine or potatoes into rounds.

Shred – This is cutting in lengths of equal and narrow width (such as a head of cabbage) with a large knife or with your grater.

Bake, Boil & Burn

... culinary metamorphosis.

Food can be eaten raw or cooked – transformed by heat. We Homo sapiens have enjoyed warm food since we discovered fire. Today we cook in many different ways.

You can use a stove top ring, an oven, a barbecue, a grill or an outdoor fire. All you need is a good heat source and something to contain the food.

Boil – 'Bring to the boil' refers to turning up the heat until the water or liquid starts to bubble. When you boil, you cook by immersing the food in hot water. Boil pasta, rice, beans, lentils, potatoes and many veggies…

Bake – Baking is done in an oven. This is a 'dry' heat. Often the food will be coated with oil or water to help transfer the heat and create a desired outer layer. Set the oven to the desired temperature, WAIT until it has reached that temperature (the thermostat indicator light goes off), then put the food in.

Where you position your tray in the oven can be important; on the higher shelf, the top side of the tray gets more heat, on the lower shelf the bottom cooks faster. Bake bread, cakes, cookies, potatoes and casseroles… and PIZZA!

Barbecue (BBQ) – Barbecuing is cooking outdoors on an open flame, the closest thing to the original primitive open fire pit. There is a certain taste from this type of cooking that is very enticing, maybe something from our past.

Blanche – Blanching involves dropping fresh vegetables in boiling water for one minute. It only slightly cooks the outer layer leaving the inside still crunchy. The veggies are removed, and cold water is poured over them to stop any further cooking. Blanched vegetables retain their colour and crunchiness. Blanching is done for vegetables used in salads, in stir fries or when freezing them for keeping.

Deep Fry – Deep frying is boiling with oil. Oil heats up to a much higher temperature than water. Cooking is faster, and the oil crisps up the outer layer of the food. Be careful when deep frying; hot oil burns badly if it splatters. Make sure food is dry before gently adding to the oil. Deep fry potatoes, samosas, falafel or thin sliced battered veggies, known as tempura.

Fry – Heat oil in an open pan. Use a vegetable oil that is stable at high temperatures such as sunflower or rapeseed oil. Olive oil is not recommended for frying; it burns at lower temperatures. Always allow it to warm up. If the oil is cold the food will soak up the oil before frying in it. You can fry most foods, and even make bread in the pan.

FRIED ONIONS

Grill – Grilling is subjecting food to direct heat; electric or by means of a gas flame, usually from the top. It is a very high heat source from one direction. When you want to crisp things or cook them fast, grill them, but you have to stay close and turn the food regularly or it will burn... Grill veggies, burgers, bread.

Roast – Roasting is cooking in the oven with food often coated in a little oil. The oil seals the food and it retains much of the flavour and juices. Heat a little oil on an oven tray then toss the food in the hot oil and spread it out, occasionally giving it a stir. Roast potatoes, garlic, almost any veggie: sweet potatoes, parsnips, pepper, tomatoes.

ROAST SPUDS

Reduce – Cooking on low heat without a lid to allow the excess water to evaporate. There are times when the dish is wet and runny, and you need to thicken it without losing the flavours. Sauces are often reduced.

SAUTÉ / STIR FRY

Sauté – Literally meaning 'hopping' in French. The food is hopped off the pan by means of regular shaking over a high heat. As you sauté, you brown the outer layer of the food using a minimum of oil. This is quick, short cooking, used when you want the food cooked on the outside yet retaining a little of the crunch. Sauté peppers, onions, courgette, mushrooms, asparagus.

Simmer – Cooking on very low heat. You may need to get the cooking started using high heat ('bring it to the boil'), then turn it down low to a simmer. Simmer soups, sauces, rice, beans.

Steam – Cooking with water, but not in water. The hot steam cooks the food. At the bottom of the pot you put a thin layer of water, maybe 1cm, and the vegetables on top; using a metal strainer, it keeps the vegetables off the bottom and out of the water. Cover the pot. Be careful that all the water does not evaporate, or the bottom will burn and we do not want that! Steam all veggies, potatoes, even rice!

Stir-fry – Frying at medium heat with a thin layer of oil, stirring regularly so food does not burn. The veggies remain crispy, only slightly cooked. Very similar to sautéing but of course in a different language! One can stir-fry most veggies.

Sweat – Frying on low heat and covered until food is just soft. Sweating onions or leeks is common.

Wilt – Cook in a little water or steam very lightly until the leaves wilt or 'melt'. When done there may be juice from the veggies, squeeze it a little to get rid of it. Generally wilting is for green leaves such as spinach, lettuce, chard or cabbage.

These blank spaces have been inserted with purpose; for your comments, other recipes, ideas... use them!

RECIPES

Recipes should be easy to follow. The fewer ingredients the better; it makes the work easier and I find the taste pure, more home-cooked. It also helps if you can find most of the ingredients in your local supermarket.

These blank spaces have been inserted with purpose; for your comments, other recipes, ideas... use them!

Soup

... of the day!

Soup is a comfort food. It is warm, easy to eat and, with a nice chunk of bread, a meal. I think soup is great any time, any season, the French influence. Make a big pot and have it for a few days… if your housemates do not eat it for you!

N.B. There is such a thing as cold soup, but that is for another time, another place, another space.

NOTE: MAKE CROUTONS
Cut old, dry or toasted bread into small squares. Sprinkle with dried herbs,
garlic powder and a drizzle of olive oil. Spread out on your tray and heat in
the oven at 100°C for 15 minutes.
Allow them to cool in order to crisp up.

POTATO & CARROT

This dish was known as a 'ragout' in my home, a big chunky vegetable stew. I have added more liquid. Using the masher, I reduce the chunks, so it is more like soup. In 15 minutes you will have great soup, can you wait that long?

Makes enough for 4 good bowls.

1 big potato – *cubed*
1 onion – *thinly chopped*
1 garlic clove – *minced*

A drop of vegetable oil
A bay leaf
A pinch of dry thyme
Enough water to cover all
Sea salt
Black pepper

1. Warm a drop of oil in your big pot and fry the onion and garlic on low heat and soften.
2. Add the potato and carrot, give it all a good stir and let it cook for another few minutes with the lid on the pot.
3. Finally, add the pinch of dried thyme, the bay leaf and enough water to cover everything.
4. Bring it to the boil and simmer for approx. 10 to 15 minutes. Check with a knife to see if the potato and carrots are cooked.
5. At the end, add a little salt and a grind of black pepper and taste it. You may want a little more salt.

If you wish, use your potato masher to reduce the vegetables and thicken the soup.

CAULIFLOWER CHOWDER

My son, who found many things difficult to eat when young, liked this soup. Perhaps it is the mild flavour and the velvety texture. It was originally known as 'white soup' in our house. We did not want him to know that it had onions or cauliflower in it!

Makes at least 6 good bowls

1 head of cauliflower – *broken into pieces*

1 large potato – *cubed*

1 onion – *finely chopped*

1 celery stalk – *finely chopped*

2 garlic cloves – *minced*

Pinch of thyme

One bay leaf

Water to cover all

Drop of vegetable oil

Sea salt

Black pepper

1. Soften the onion, the celery and the garlic in the drop of oil on low heat. This will only take a few minutes. Keep the pot covered.
2. Then add the potato and cook for another 5 minutes, stirring from time to time so nothing burns.
3. Add the cauliflower, the pinch of thyme, the bay leaf and enough water to cover it all.
4. Bring to the boil then simmer for another 10 minutes. You want the potato and the cauliflower to be soft.
5. Season with ½ tsp of salt and a grind of black pepper.

A potato masher will reduce it to a thick chunky soup. If you have a blender, that 'bullet', you can make it real smoooooooth, pure white and velvety – do not forget to remove the bay leaf before blending.

SOUPE VERTE *Green soup*

Soupe Verte – French for green soup. Handed down from generation to generation in my mother's family. This was and is our family's cure-all. It was made whenever anyone was sick. If a little run-down or weak, no better medicine! After a flu, one bowl of this soup and we would jump out of bed! A wonderful combination of green vegetables. When blended it turns a wonderful life-affirming colour of green.

Makes enough for 6 to 8 bowls.

1 large leek – *finely chopped*
2 garlic cloves – *minced*
1 celery stick – *finely chopped*
1 zucchini/courgette – *cubed*
1 cup of any other greens – *optional*

Pinch of thyme
2 bay leaves
Water to cover the vegetables
½ cup of fresh parsley
Drop of vegetable oil
Sea salt

1. Cut the leek in two along the length and rinse well under running water to remove any sand between the layers.
2. In your big pot soften the leek, the celery and the garlic on a low heat.
3. Add the other chopped vegetables, the pinch of thyme, the bay leaves and enough water to cover it all. Bring to a boil and simmer for another 10 minutes until all is soft but still bright green.
4. Finely chop the parsley and add it at the end. Season with salt to taste.
5. Allow to cool a little then blend it to make a smooth bright green soup or serve chunky. Remember to remove the bay leaf before blending.

If the soup seems too thick add a bit more water.

TOMATO

This tomato soup is light and very flavoursome, almost refreshing! If you are lucky enough to live in a region where tomatoes ripen naturally, use fresh ones, otherwise canned tomatoes are available all year round.

Makes enough for 6 to 8 bowls

1 onion – *finely chopped*
1 celery stick – *finely chopped*
2 garlic cloves – *minced*
2 tins of tomatoes, 800g – *roughly chopped*
(or 3 cups or 8 medium fresh tomatoes)
5 cups of water
A few springs of fresh basil
Drop of vegetable oil
Pinch of thyme
1 bay leaf
Sea salt
Black pepper

1. Soften the onion, the celery and the garlic in a drop of vegetable oil on low heat.
2. Add the tomatoes, the pinch of thyme and the bay leaf. Let it all cook for 5 minutes before adding the water.
3. Bring it to the boil then simmer for 10 minutes. Taste it first, add a little salt if needed; sometimes canned tomatoes already have a good bit of salt.
4. Remove the bay leaf before blending it.

Top with a little chopped fresh basil and freshly ground black pepper.

CALABAZA *Squash*

The Calabaza means butternut squash to Latin Americans. There are different varieties and colours. The most popular in our shops is the beige oversized pear-shaped gourd.

Makes enough for 4 good bowls.

1 butternut squash – *deseeded, peeled & cubed*
1 onion – *thinly chopped*
1 carrot – *chopped small*
1 celery stick – *chopped small*
1 garlic clove – *minced*

Drop of vegetable oil
A bay leaf
A pinch of dry thyme
Enough water to cover all
Sea salt
Black pepper

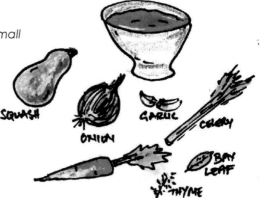

1. Warm a drop of oil in your big pot and soften the onion, the celery and garlic on a low heat.
2. Add the carrot and the squash. Give it all a good stir and let it cook for another few minutes with the lid on the pot.
3. Finally, add the pinch of dried thyme, the bay leaf, and enough water to cover everything.
4. Bring it to the boil then simmer for approx. 10 to 15 minutes. Check with a knife to see if the carrots and squash are cooked.
5. At the end add a little salt and a grind of black pepper. Stir well and taste it, you may want a little more.

This soup will turn out bright orange and velvety.

SPICY KIDNEY BEAN

I found this recipe in a children's cookbook.* When things are explained in simple ways for young children, even I can understand! Once I started making it, the hungry older college students in the house requested it… often. The chilli and warm hearty beans combined with a little fresh coriander is addictive.

Makes enough for 6 or 4 hungry people.

1 red onion – *finely chopped*
1 celery stick – *finely chopped*
2 garlic cloves – *finely chopped*
1 400g tin tomatoes
1 400g tin kidney beans – *rinsed*

½ tsp chilli powder
½ tsp ground coriander
½ tsp ground cumin
2 cups of water
½ cup chopped fresh coriander
Sea salt & black pepper

1. Soften the onion, the celery and the garlic in a drop of vegetable oil.
2. Add the spices, chilli, coriander, cumin, and stir well.
3. After a minute add the tomatoes, the kidney beans and the water. Bring it to the boil then simmer for 15 minutes.
4. Allow it to cool for a few minutes then blend it well, it will become velvety smooth.

Taste it and add a little salt, a grind of black pepper and the fresh chopped coriander just before serving.

Gilpin, R. and Patchett, F. (2007), The Usborne Cookbook for Children, Usborne Publishing Ltd, London, pp.16–17 – recipe from Catherine Atkinson

These blank spaces have been inserted with purpose; for your comments, other recipes, ideas... use them!

Salad

Salad gives life and energy. When you are tired, but you want something to eat, have green leaf salad – easy on the digestive system and full of vitamins!

Fresh, vibrant, full of brain food. Salads are easy and quick – a little cleaning, a bit of chopping, a splatter of dressing and you have a meal. The dressing can be as simple as a squeeze of lemon and a drizzle of olive oil.

VINAIGRETTE ... *French salad dressing*

Vinaigrette is a basic vinegar-based French dressing that goes with almost all salads; on greens, on tomatoes, on potatoes or perfect as a dip for warm bread

Makes enough for a week of salads.

½ cup olive oil
¼ cup apple cider vinegar
1 tsp Dijon mustard
1 or 2 garlic cloves – *minced*
A pinch of salt

1. Put all the ingredients together into a jar, screw the lid on tight and shake until all the ingredients are well mixed.

OLIVE OIL

APPLE CIDER VINEGAR

GARLIC

SALT

DIJON MUSTARD

Some may prefer to leave out the garlic, I add even more, 4 or 5 cloves. It is a matter of taste. Give it a good shake every time before using as the oil and vinegar may separate. When kept in the fridge the olive oil will solidify. Take it out for 10 minutes before using. Keeps fresh in the fridge for over a week.

GREEN LEAVES

The first salad I was introduced to at our family's table was lettuce salad. When I hear the word 'salad', green leaves is the first thing I think about. There are many types: romaine, cos, Boston, rocket, Spinach; the availability depends on where you live. Some are crisp, others soft, dark green, curly. At times I only use one type, at other times I mix several together, it usually depends on what I have in the fridge.

Makes enough for 4 as a side salad.

½ **head of lettuce** – *washed and torn into small pieces*
¼ **red onion** – *finely chopped*

2 tbsp fresh parsley – *finely chopped*
2 to 3 tbsp of vinaigrette

1. In your serving bowl marinate the onions with 2 or 3 tablespoons of vinaigrette for a few minutes.
2. Tear the washed and dried leaves into smaller pieces as you add them to the bowl.
3. Give it a good mix so all the leaves get well coated.

GREEN LEAF SALAD

GRATED CARROT

So simple – only grated carrots and a little dressing. I serve it any time and with most things when I need a refreshing salad to complete a meal. Perfect to accompany pizza. The wonderful bright orange colour adds to the presentation on your plate, most importantly!

Enough for 4 to 6 as a side salad.

3 big carrots *– coarsely grated*

2 tbsp olive oil
1 tbsp apple cider vinegar
1 tsp lemon juice
Fresh parsley (if available)
Sea salt

1. Peel and grate your carrots. There are several sizes of holes on your grater. I prefer the larger size; you decide. The different sizes give a different texture, and I think a different taste.
2. Add the oil, the vinegar and the lemon juice and mix it well.

If you like, sprinkle a little chopped parsley on top.

AVOCADO

The easiest way to eat an avocado is to cut it in half, remove the stone and fill the hole with vinaigrette. Scoop out the flesh with a spoon, one bite at a time – my dear wife Carmel's favourite way to eat avocado, no preparation required. You can also make a mixed salad with avocado, eat it the civilised way – my way!

Makes enough for 4 diners

2 avocados – *flesh chopped into large chunks*
1 tomato – *roughly chopped*
1 small shallot – *finely chopped*

Coriander – *finely chopped*
Juice of ½ lemon
Sea salt

1. Combine the avocado, the tomato, the shallot, the coriander, the lemon juice and a sprinkle of salt.
2. Mix together gently so the avocado does not break apart.

Use ONLY ripe avocados!

To check if the avocado is ripe give it a little squeeze with your thumb, the flesh should yield to the touch… like so many good things in life.

CABBAGE

Plain cabbage salad was regularly on the menu at home. I added the carrot and onion and I think it works very well! Fresh cabbage with a little carrot for colour and onion to round off the taste. The oil and vinegar dressing is light. I prepare it ahead of the meal and allow it to marinate. The cabbage will soften a little.

Makes enough for 6.

½ **cabbage** – *chopped in fine strips*
1 **carrot** – *grated*
¼ **sweet or red onion** – *in fine strips*

3 tbsp olive oil
2 tbsp apple cider vinegar
A pinch of sea salt
A grind or two of black pepper

1. Remove any discoloured leaves of cabbage and cut out the central core. Using your big knife, slowly chop off fine strips of cabbage until all done.
2. Add the grated carrot, the strips of onion, the oil and the vinegar.
3. Sprinkle a little salt and a grind of black pepper over it.
4. Mix together well and taste it. It may need a little more vinegar, oil or salt.

Allow to stand in the fridge for 20 minutes before serving.

TOMATO & RED ONION

I first tasted this salad aboard a pleasure sailing craft somewhere in the Mediterranean. Fred, the resident chef, served it along with home-fired potatoes, a large goblet of red wine and plenty of baguette. I always made tomato salad with garlic, but the addition of the red onions gives it something sweet and strong in flavour. It will be popular so make enough of it.

Makes enough for 4 diners.

2 or 3 tomatoes – *cut into wedges*
1 red onion – *sliced into strips*
1 garlic clove – *minced*

4 tbsp olive oil
4 tbsp cider vinegar
A pinch of sea salt

1. Mix all the ingredients together and set aside to marinate for 10 minutes before serving. The time allows the onion and garlic to lose some of their overpowering taste.

Use more oil and vinegar if you like. Once the salad is eaten the remaining juice in the bowl is perfect for dipping your bread into.

CUCUMBER DILL

Dill is used a lot in central Europe. It has to be fresh dill or it will have no taste. This is a mild tasting salad that goes well when you need a good refreshing side dish.

Enough for 4 to 6 as a side salad.

1 cucumber – *sliced into rounds*
A few strands of chives – *finely chopped*
Fresh dill – *finely chopped*

2 tbsp olive oil
1 tsp lemon juice
Sea salt

1. Wash the cucumber then slice into thin rounds.
2. Mix together the oil, the lemon juice, the chives and the dill.

Allow to rest 20 minutes in the fridge before serving.

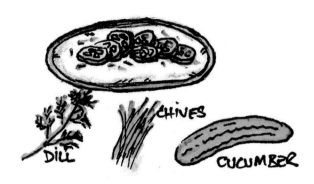

LEAVES & BEANS

My friend, Frank, came into my house and gave me this recipe. He called it a 'G-Bomb' – greens, beans, onion, mushrooms, berries and seeds. I omitted the berries in my recipe because I have never liked fruit in salad, and it is my book, my way… unless of course it is fruit salad. This dish is a complete meal. Perfect for lunch all by itself.

Makes enough for 4 diners.

Bunch of green leaves – *washed*
½ cup black/kidney beans – *minced*
¼ red onion – *sliced into strips*
5 mushrooms – *sliced*
Small handful toasted seeds – sunflower
2 or more tbsp of vinaigrette

1. Wash and dry your greens.
2. Drain the beans and rinse well.
3. Combine the greens, the beans, the onion and the mushrooms with the vinaigrette and mix well.
4. Sprinkle the toasted seeds as you serve.

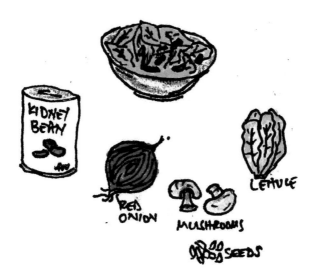

MEXICAN

When I feel the need for something hearty yet vibrant and great tasting, I make this. Bring it to a gathering and your status as the 'chef' will go up! This you can eat on a pile of green leaves to make it a meal, served as a side salad with your burritos or alone with a big pile of nachos.

Makes enough for 6 as an accompanying dish or 4 as a lunch dish served on a bed of green leaves.

1 can kidney beans – *drained and rinsed*
1 can of corn kernels – *drained and rinsed*
1 red pepper – *chopped small*
1 clove of garlic – *minced*
½ sweet or red onion – *finely chopped*
1 ripe avocado – *cubed*
4 tbsp coriander – *finely chopped*

1 tsp ground cumin
½ tsp chilli flakes
2 tbsp olive oil
Juice of one lime
½ tsp of sea salt

1. Empty the cans of beans and corn into a colander and rinse under the tap. Drain well.
2. In a large bowl, mix everything together. Do not over mix.
3. Taste it to see if it might need a little more lime juice or salt.

Allow to rest in the fridge for a half hour before serving.

BROCCOLI & HAZELNUTS

My friend Teresa's house parties always involve great food. One salad that I always like is blanched broccoli, cherry tomatoes and hazelnuts. It is one of the first to disappear. I often want seconds but the bowl empties quickly! I have tried to reproduce her wonderful work, my way!

Makes enough for 4 to 6 as a side salad.

½ **head of broccoli** – *broken into bitesize florets*
½ **red onion** – *cut into fine strips*
1 **garlic clove** – *finely chopped*
1 **cup of cherry tomatoes** – *left whole*
1 **red bell pepper** – *in thin strips*
½ **cup of hazelnuts** – *roasted and skins removed*

2 **tbsp fresh parsley** – *finely chopped*
2 **tbsp of olive oil**
Juice of one lemon
Sea salt

1. To blanche the broccoli florets, put them into your big bowl and pour boiling water over them. Allow to sit for 2 minutes and drain off the water.
2. Add the other ingredients and mix well.
3. Season and allow to rest in the fridge for 20 minutes before serving.

NOTE: To remove the skins off the hazelnuts, roast them for 5 minutes in a hot oven; do not let them burn. Allow to cool then rub the nuts between your hands and the skins easily break off.

These blank pages have been inserted with purpose; for your comments, other recipes, ideas... use them!

Le Sandwich

We all know how to make a sandwich, even if it is only peanut butter and jam (and don't knock that one, it is a classic).

What we generally need are ideas, and a little creativity. For me the key is to load it up. Make sure you put on enough filling that it is the dominant taste, even if some of it falls out while you are eating!

HUMMUS & ROASTED RED PEPPERS

Hummus makes a good foundation to any topping and the roasted red pepper goes very well with it. A good choice of bread for this sandwich is a sliced bread loaf which is firm yet not too strong in flavour such as **light sourdough**, a popular polish bread.

Makes one sandwich each!

4 tbsp Hummus (p. 78)
4 to 6 roasted red pepper slices
Handful of rocket leaves
Grind of black pepper

1. Spread a nice layer of hummus on each slice. You can buy a tub of it or make some yourself, see p.78
2. Cover the hummus with a few strips of roasted red pepper* and a layer of rocket leaves.
3. Grind a little black pepper on the other slice and 'sandwich' them together.

> *Roasted red pepper can come from a jar, but it is easy to make it yourself. Cut the pepper in half, remove the core and place under a hot grill skin side up. When the skin turns black, allow it to cool a little, remove the skin and use as wished... made at home tastes amazing!*

HOT MUSHROOM

This is a warm sandwich. It will take a little effort to eat; hold it tight so everything doesn't fall out. You may have a mess on your hands before it is finished but it is worth it! Use good **firm bread rolls** or **ciabatta.**

Makes one sandwich each!

1 large portobello mushroom
½ garlic clove – *minced*
2 tbsp ground almonds or breadcrumbs
A few lettuce leaves
3 or 4 slices of tomato

½ tsp dried oregano
A little Dijon mustard
A scoop of vegan mayo
1 tsp olive oil
Pinch of sea salt
Grind of black pepper

1. Remove the stem and place the mushroom upside down on your tray.
2. Finely chop the stem and mix with the garlic, ground almonds/breadcrumbs, oregano, salt and pepper.
3. Fill the mushroom 'cup' with the dry mixture and drizzle the olive oil over it.
4. Cook in a pre-heated oven at 200°C/400°F for approx. 10 minutes. Check if it has softened but remains a little firm.
5. Slice the roll in two. On one side spread a little Dijon mustard and place the hot mushroom on it, then the lettuce and the tomato slices. On the other side spread a layer of vegan mayo and press together.

Make sure the mushrooms are fresh – bright cream on top and light brown gills underneath.

AVOCADO & TOMATO

Ripe avocado and tomato are a great combination – wonderful colour and great taste! Use good **sourdough bread** if you can get it. But any good sliced bread will be good.

Makes one sandwich each!

1 ripe avocado – *stone and skin removed*
1 ripe tomato – *sliced in rounds*
½ **clove of garlic** – *sliced very thin*

Pinch of chilli flakes
A tsp of coriander – *finely chopped*
A scoop of vegan mayo
A grind of black pepper

AVOCADO & TOMATO

1. Split the avocado in two, take out the stone, peel it and slice it up.
2. Cover one slice of bread with a thick layer of avocado and a light pinch of salt and chilli flakes.
3. Spread out a few slices of tomato, fresh garlic shavings and a grind of black pepper.
4. Cover the other slice with a layer of vegan mayo and press together.

You can also add red onion, lettuce or rocket. Be creative and follow your own taste.

CUCUMBER

I remember my Aunt Mary making these for my Uncle Ray. I was always fascinated by this sandwich made with only one vegetable, two slices of bread and a thick layer of cucumber slices well lathered in mayonnaise… and don't forget, plenty of black pepper. At that time the field cucumbers were shorter, had tough skins but had plenty of flavour. Today we find long ones with thin skins and no seeds but the taste is milder. I like to use **slices of white soft bread**; it goes well with the mild cucumber taste.

Makes one sandwich each!

1 cucumber – *sliced in rounds*
4 tbsp vegan mayo (p. 113)

Pinch of sea salt
A grind of black pepper

1. Slather vegan mayo on both slices of bread.
2. If you are using the long cucumbers, just wash and use with the skins. If you are using the shorter fatter variety the skins can be tough. I would remove the skin and if the seeds are big, remove them as well.
3. Cover one slice of bread with a thick layer of cucumber slices. Sprinkle a little salt over them and a grind of black pepper.
4. Press the other slice of bread on top and eat.

GRILLED VEGGIES

I often have leftover toppings from pizza night. One Saturday morning we were going for a drive to the sea and, as is my way, I made a big picnic to bring along. Finding the toppings in the fridge I stuffed them into crispy bread; aubergine slices, courgette, some grilled red pepper. When we stopped for a break I produced the sambos. The taste was amazing... if I say so myself! Crunchy **baguette** works well, it is strong enough to hold plenty of grilled veggies.

With a long baguette you can make 3 or 4 sandwiches.

1 aubergine/eggplant – *sliced 5mm thick*
1 zucchini/courgette – *sliced*
1 red pepper – *deseeded and cut into chunks*
1 onion in rounds
3 cloves of garlic – *intact (with the skins on)*

1 tsp dried oregano
Drizzle of olive oil

1. Put the chopped veggies in your big bowl, drizzle a little olive oil over them and mix well.
2. Spread them out on a tray and place in the hot oven, approx. 200°C/400°F for 15–20 minutes, turning once after 10 minutes.
3. Check to see if the garlic is soft. Remove tray from the oven and sprinkle with a little dried oregano, a drizzle of olive oil and a pinch of sea salt.
4. Squeeze the garlic from the skins and spread on one side of the bread. Stuff as many veggies as you like into the sandwich.

CREAM (VEGAN CHEESE) SPREAD & LETTUCE

The cream cheese I recommend is made from coconut oil, a bit of starch and a few other ingredients – purely plant-based. At one time this could only be found in health food stores, but today many supermarkets carry it because of its popularity and because it tastes very good. Any bread works well, whatever you have in the kitchen at the time.

Makes one big sandwich.

2 tbsp coconut cream spread/vegan cheese
1 tbsp spring onion – *chopped finely*
½ garlic clove – *minced*
Good grind of black pepper

4 large lettuce leaves – *washed*
A slice of tomato or two

1. Mix the cream spread with the spring onion, garlic and ground black pepper.
2. Spread the cream spread over one slice of bread.
3. Cover with a few lettuce leaves and a slice or two of tomato.
4. Place the other slice of bread on top and eat!

These blank pages have been inserted with purpose; for your comments, other recipes, ideas... use them!

Pasta

Pasta was, in my time, the college student's subsistence diet; very easy and very quick to make and, perhaps most importantly, very cheap. At the end of the month when the money ran out, there was always enough for a bag of pasta and a jar of tomato sauce.

How to cook pasta?

1. Bring a big pot of water to the boil.
2. Toss in the pasta and stir well.
3. Most dry pasta cooks in approx. 10 minutes.

For more detail, turn to page 150.

A jar of sauce is fine, but why not something fresh, homemade, tasty… and so easy?!

SWEET TOMATO

I always made my tomato sauce without chunks, everything finely chopped. Carmel, my housemate, started making sauce using a lot of onion coarsely chopped. The sauce was chunky and slightly sweet; I liked it. Now it is my sauce, my classic!

Makes 2 to 3 portions or 4 starter plates.

Any Pasta will do! 250g/8oz – I like shells
1 400g tin plum tomatoes – *whole tomatoes*
1 big sweet onion – *coarsely chopped*
1 clove garlic – *minced*

½ tsp of dried oregano
A grind of black pepper
Olive oil

1. Chop the onion into 1cm/½ chunks or bigger.
2. Warm the oil, soften the onion and garlic on a very low heat, covered.
3. Empty the tinned tomatoes into a bowl and mash with your potato masher.
4. Add tomatoes and the dried oregano to the onion.
5. Simmer without the lid for 10 to 15 minutes. Taste it; perhaps a pinch of salt may be necessary.
6. Cook your pasta. Once al dente, drain and add it to the sauce and re-heat all together.

Serve with plenty of fresh ground pepper on top.

SPICY MUSHROOM

Recipes come to you when you most need them. I found this recipe on a flyer in a supermarket. I made it while wooing a young lady. Is it not said: "a way to a woman's heart is via her stomach"? If you cook well, resistance is futile! Better than a guitar! It is now one of our favourite pasta dishes, and she is still around! Spicy, smoky, and oily... the sauce of course!

Makes 3 nice portions or 5 starter dishes.

Penne Pasta – *two handfuls, 250g/8oz*
1 400g tin plum tomatoes – *whole tomatoes*
Big handfuls of button mushrooms,
the smaller the better – *cleaned & whole*
10 cloves of garlic
½ tsp of chilli flakes, more if you like
¼ cup of olive oil

1. In your pot, heat the olive oil on low heat. Once the oil is warm add the mushrooms whole and allow them to brown and the juices to flow. Pour out the liquid and keep.*
2. Add chilli flakes and the garlic cloves, peeled but whole.
3. Simmer uncovered for 5 minutes.
4. As the garlic softens, add the tin of tomatoes and cook for another 5 minutes.
5. Season with salt.
6. Cook your pasta. Once al dente, drain, add it to the sauce and re-heat all together.

Nothing better to warm things up... I know!!!

> *NOTE: The liquid from the mushrooms is an elixir reserved only for the chef. Allow to cool and drink, or soak your bread in it.*

GARLIC & PARSLEY

Garlic is wonderful in/on almost anything. Liam, my cousin, was visiting us and offered to cook us a pasta dish with lots of garlic. It is rare that I retreat from my sacred space, but he showed confidence, so I stepped back. It was good to observe a fellow culinary aficionado go about his work. I picked up a new recipe!

Makes enough for 3 hungry individuals.

Fettuccine Pasta – *two handfuls, 250g/8oz*
5+ cloves of garlic – *sliced*
3 tbsp olive oil
½ tsp of chilli flakes
1 cup of pasta water

½ cup fresh parsley – *finely chopped*
Sea salt
A good grind of fresh black pepper

1. Bring the water for your pasta to the boil and toss in the pasta.
2. As the pasta is cooking, warm your pan with the olive oil – low heat only. Add the garlic and the chilli. Soften the garlic, a minute or two will be enough.*
3. Chop the parsley and set aside.
4. Once the pasta is al dente, drain, keeping a cup of the water.
5. Add the pasta to the chilli and garlic and 1/2 a cup of the water. Turn up the heat and stir all together for a minute or two.
6. Once nice and warm mix in the parsley, a pinch of salt and a good grind of black pepper.

> *NOTE: In some cooking culture, the garlic is removed, only the essence remaining in the oil... but why?!*

BASIL PESTO

Homemade pesto takes a little work but there is no cooking required. The fresh vibrant flavour is amazing. Once you taste it, you won't believe you made it yourself! Our young child, Anne Marie, practically lives off it. She comes home hungry from school and instead of toast she cooks herself a bowl of pasta and smothers it with a big dollop of pesto. I like to use linguine pasta because when I first ate fresh homemade pesto it was with linguine. I still make it that way today… a terrible habit!

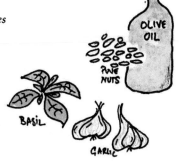

Makes 2 good portions or 4 starter dishes

Linguine pasta – *160g/6oz*
2 cups fresh basil leaves – *finely chopped*
2 garlic cloves – *minced*
¼ cup pine nuts – *finely chopped*

¼ cup olive oil
½ cup cooking water
Sea salt

1. With your big sharp knife mince the garlic, the basil leaves and the pine nuts at the same time until it is almost a paste. You may need to do this in several small batches.
2. In your large bowl mix the basil with enough olive oil and a pinch of salt to make a runny sauce – presto, pesto! … Sorry!!!
3. Cook the linguine until it is al dente and drain the water, retaining a ½ cup.
4. Put the pasta back in the pot, add a few tablespoons of pesto and a little of the original water to make it wet and mix well, you want the pasta very well coated.
5. Heat it up for a minute and turn off the heat.

Toast a few pine nuts in the oven till they start to brown, sprinkle over the pasta as you serve.

ROAST VEGGIES

I am not sure why I do not make these dishes more often, no work – a rinse, a chop, into the oven and wait. The roasting allows the water to evaporate, the flavours are concentrated and strong. I always make sure there is plenty of garlic – roast garlic makes the dish!

Makes enough for 2 hungry individuals

Penne pasta 2 big handfuls 250g/8oz)
1 red pepper – *cubed*
5 cloves garlic – *peeled and whole*
½ courgette/zucchini – *cubed*
1 onion – *coarsely chopped*
¼ cup white wine

A drizzle of olive oil
A pinch of sea salt

1. Pre-heat the oven to 180°C/380°F.
2. Mix all the veggies together and spread out on your oven tray. Give them 20 minutes, stirring once or twice, then turn off the heat.
3. Drizzle a little olive oil over them, mix well and allow to cool.
4. Cook your pasta. Once al dente, drain and set aside.
5. Put the veggies in a warm frying pan along with the white wine. After a minute mix in the pasta.

Serve hot.

These blank pages have been inserted with purpose; for your comments, other recipes, ideas... use them!

Stir-Fry

I was in a restaurant recently eating a lively, crispy, stir-fried dish and really enjoyed the freshness. Stir-fry dishes we made regularly when we were younger but for some reason they have gone 'out of fashion' in our cooking.

I looked across the table at my dining mate and before I could say anything she blurted out, "do you think you should have a stir-fry in the cookbook?" … I do now, thanks Carmel.

Stir-Fry Kit ...*regular ingredients used in a stir-fry:*

- Tamari (soy sauce)
- Toasted sesame seed oil
- Fresh garlic, ginger & coriander
- Limes

CARMEL'S RICE & TOFU

From time to time we would have a big pot of cooked rice left over from the night before. Perfect time to make this recipe. The rice with all the veggies and the sauce is delicious… there is never any of this left over!

Makes enough for 4 or 3 hungry individuals.

1 onion – *finely chopped*

2 cloves of garlic – *sliced*

1 thumb-size piece of ginger – *finely chopped*

1 big carrot – *cut into matchsticks*

½ cup fresh peas – *unthawed if frozen*

1 250g block of firm tofu – *cut into cubes*

2 cups cooked brown rice

Tofu Marinade

1 tbsp of tamari/soy sauce

2 cloves of garlic

1 thumb-size piece of ginger – *finely chopped*

1. If you do not have any left over rice, cook some ahead of time, you want it cold.
2. Marinate your tofu for at least half an hour.
3. Stir-fry the onion, garlic, ginger and carrots. Once the carrots are almost soft add the peas and cook for another few minutes.
4. Mix in the rice and the marinade from the tofu and heat together.
5. At the same time fry the tofu cubes till brown. Serve with the rice mixture.

You may like to drizzle a little sesame oil over everything and sprinkle with fresh chopped coriander as you serve it.

GREENS & CASHEWS

Sometimes I like to use only one colour of vegetables. Perhaps it is the concentration of chlorophyll, but it gives the dish a unique flavour and wonderful colour. The cashews is the contrast.

Makes enough for 2 hungry individuals.

2 spring onions – *chopped in angled rounds*
1 cup broccoli – *florets*
1 courgette/zucchini – *cut in short strips*
1 green pepper – *cut into strips*
½ cup whole cashews – *toasted*

1 thumb-size piece of ginger – *finely chopped*
1 clove of garlic – *sliced*
1 tbsp tamari/soy sauce
¼ cup fresh parsley – *finely chopped*
1 tbsp lime juice

Brown or white rice – **½ cup uncooked**

1. If using good brown rice, it can take up to 40 minutes, so put it on first. See page …
2. In a dry frying pan, toast the cashews until just starting to brown, set aside and allow to cool.
3. Prepare all the ingredients and have them ready.
4. If you have a wok great, if not, a pan will work well. Heat the pan on medium heat, drizzle a tablespoon of vegetable oil into it, then add the veggies – start with the pepper, the broccoli and the courgette. After another minute or two introduce the garlic, the spring onions and the ginger, along with the tamari soy sauce. Keep stirring all the time so nothing burns.
5. Once the veggies are slightly cooked but still crisp remove from the heat. Mix in the cashews, the parsley and the lime juice.

Serve on a bed of rice.

MUSHROOMS & KALE

Kale has become quite popular in fashionable culinary circles, maybe something to do with it being 'high in vitamin C'. I like the strong taste and texture; even after cooking, there is something to chew on.

Makes enough for 3.

2 spring onions – *chopped in angled rounds*
1 large handful mushrooms – *sliced*
1 bunch of kale – *centre rib removed, cut into strips*
1 tbsp sesame seeds – *toasted*

1 thumb-size piece of ginger – *finely chopped*
1 clove of garlic – *sliced*
1 tbsp tamari/soy sauce
1 tbsp toasted sesame oil
2 tbsp lime juice

Rice noodles – *A handful, 150g/5oz*

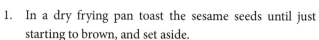

1. In a dry frying pan toast the sesame seeds until just starting to brown, and set aside.
2. Fry the mushrooms in a drop of oil until starting to sweat, take off the heat, stir in 1 tbsp of the lime juice and a dash of salt and set aside.
3. Fry the chopped kale in your pan with a drop of water on medium heat until just starting to soften and set aside.
4. To make the sauce, mix together the garlic, the spring onions and the ginger along with the tamari soy sauce and heat for a minute.
5. Cook the noodles until al dente.
6. Transfer the noodles to the pan of sauce along with the mushrooms and the kale, heat through for 1 minute or 2.
7. At the end add the sesame seeds, the remaining tbsp of lime juice and tbsp of sesame seed oil. Mix together and serve.

SWEET, SOUR & TOFU

I am often told tofu has no taste, which is true until you marinate it or fry or roast it. The Asian community make the most wonderful foods with this soya bean curd – much too advanced for this volume, or me! Here is my version of crispy, tasty tofu and lively veggies.

Makes enough for 3 hungry individuals.

2 cloves of garlic *– sliced*
5 or 6 small bok choy bunches *– trimmed only*
1 big carrot *– cut into strips*
1 red pepper *– cut into strips*
1 250g/8oz block of soft tofu *– cubed*

½ cup fresh coriander *– chopped*
½ cup of sweet & sour sauce, *(p. 115)*

Rice noodles *– two handfuls 150g/5oz*

1. To prepare the tofu – coat the cubes in a little vegetable oil and place on a tray in a hot oven, 200°C. You will need to turn them once or twice so they are brown and crisp evenly, then set aside.
2. Put the pan or wok over a medium heat, drizzle a little oil and toss in the carrots, then the peppers. After a minute add the bok choy and the garlic.
3. Cook for another minute or two.
4. Add the tofu cubes and the sauce and allow it to come together for 2 or 3 minutes.
5. Cook the noodles. Once al dente transfer to veggies and warm together.
6. Mix in the fresh coriander and serve.

LEMONGRASS & CHILLI

Lemongrass, lime juice and a nice bit of chilli go very well together. For this I keep the soy sauce apart, its flavour overpowering. The lemongrass is subtle. I serve this with satay, coated tofu squares on the side. The two have very different flavours, I like a bit of each.

Makes enough for 4.

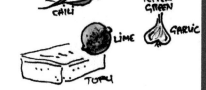

2 spring onions – *chopped in rounds*
1 red pepper – *cut into fine strips*
1 green pepper – *cut into fine strips*
2 red chillies – *finely sliced, seeds removed*
1 handful of mange-tout
1 stem of lemongrass – *very finely chopped*
3 cloves of garlic – *sliced*
2 tbsp lime juice

1 250g/8oz block of firm tofu – *cubed*
½ cup satay peanut sauce *(p. 114)*

Rice noodles – *two handfuls, 150g/5oz*

1. Prepare the tofu. It takes a bit of time. Coat the cubes in a little vegetable oil and place on a tray in a hot oven at 200°C. You will need to turn them once or twice so they are brown and crisp evenly. Set aside.
2. Heat the pan on a medium heat, drizzle a little vegetable oil onto it and toss in the peppers and chilli. After a minute add the mange-tout, the spring onion, the garlic and the lemongrass. Cook for another minute and turn off the heat.
3. In a pot of water, cook the noodles and transfer to the veggies. Keep a cup of the water.
4. Warm the satay sauce and mix in the tofu cubes.
5. Add ½ cup of the water and warm everything together.

Serve with tofu squares in satay sauce on the side.

These blank pages have been inserted with purpose; for your comments, other recipes, ideas... use them!

My Soul Food

These dishes are my 'Soul Foods', I make them all the time.

Bruschetta, I make every time I arrive home hungry... which is most of the time. Hummus, the fridge is never without. Guacamole, made most Fridays, if not more often, whenever the avocados are ripe. Refried beans are always on the stove.

BRUSCHETTA

Bruschetta is toasted bread with some type of topping that usually involves garlic and olive oil: wonderful. Crispy baguette or Italian crusty loaf works well – cut slices 1cm/½ thick or a little thicker and toast both sides. But any toasted bread will do, even pitta – great to scoop up the filling. My older daughter, Isabelle, would walk into my kitchen after being away. On seeing the plate of bruschetta she would grab a piece, take a bite and exclaim, "Hmmm, I missed that."

Each topping recipe makes enough for 4 big slices of toasted bread.

1 big handful of cherry tomatoes – *quartered*
1 clove of garlic – *minced*
A few leaves of fresh basil
1 or 2 tbsp olive oil
Pinch of salt

BASIL

TOMATOES

EXTRA VIRGIN OLIVE OIL

GARLIC

TOMATO BRUSCHETTA – il Classico

1. Mix the cherry tomatoes and the garlic together. Drizzle the olive oil over it and the pinch of salt. Tear up the basil and mix it in.
2. Toast the bread, allow to cool and cover it with the tomato mixture.

RED WINE

Optional ☺

PAN TOMAQUET – Catalan

1 tomato – *cut in two*
1 clove of garlic – *peeled & whole*
A drizzle of olive oil
Sea salt

1. Toast the bread; a heavy white sourdough type works well. Give it a good rub with the garlic clove, do the same with the ½ tomato then drizzle with olive oil and a good sprinkle of sea salt.

My first taste of this bread was having lunch in Barcelona. I was given the garlic, the tomato, the olive oil and the toasted bread – I was to make it myself!

AVOCADO BRUSCHETTA – à la Horan

1 ripe avocado – *mashed*
1 small tomato – *chopped small*
1 clove of garlic – *minced*
2 tbsp lemon juice
Olive oil

1. Toast ciabatta bread.
2. Mash the avocado, mix in the lemon juice and a little salt, and set aside.
3. Separately chop the tomato and the garlic and mix with a little olive oil.
4. On your bread, spread a thick layer of the avocado then a good scoop of tomato mixture.

This was presented to me while dining at my friend Paddy's table – the combination of flavours is still memorable.

HUMMUS

Hummus was not included in the book until Maeve started editing the book for me and spoke up: "The one thing I noticed is that the hummus recipe is missing (oh, the horror!!)". I quickly added it, thanks Maeve! The word hummus in Arabic means chickpeas. Hummus is great as a dip for raw veggies, eaten warm with flat bread, as a sandwich spread, or on the side with your meal; I eat it with everything. A daily staple in our house.

Makes enough for 4 people.

1 tin of chickpeas – *drained and rinsed*
1 tbsp of tahini
1 garlic clove – *minced*
1 tbsp lemon juice

1 to 2 tbsp olive oil
¼ cup of water
½ tsp ground cumin
¼ tsp sea salt

1. Mash the chickpeas with a fork or with your potato masher until they are as smooth as possible.
2. Add the other ingredients and mix well… ready.

Yes, that's it!

Hummus can be made with any variety of flavours by adding sun-dried tomatoes, roasted red peppers, chilli or spring onion, anything you like.

Those with a food processor can make the hummus very smooth – blend it all together with a little more water and oil – done.

HUMMUS

GUACAMOLE

Ripe avocado is ambrosia – food of the gods! The flesh of the avocado has a creamy texture. When you mash it, it turns into a natural paste; add a few ingredients and you have a lively dip – guacamole: avocado sauce in Mexican. Perfect with nachos and an ideal companion to the burrito.

Makes enough for 4 people as a dip.

2 ripe avocados – *skin and stone removed*
1 clove of garlic – *minced*
1 tomato – *seeds removed & finely chopped*
½ a fresh hot chilli – *finely chopped*
2 tbsp coriander – *finely chopped*
½ red onion – *finely chopped*

2 tbsp lime juice
Sea salt
Black pepper

1. Mash the avocado flesh with a fork.
2. Mix in the rest – the garlic, the lime juice, the tomato, the chilli, the red onion and the cilantro.
3. Taste and add a bit of salt and pepper if required.
4. Allow to rest in the fridge for 20 minutes before serving.

Only use ripe avocados. You want them soft. Press them with your thumb; if they give, they are ripe. Unripe avocados are horrible, hard and tasteless.

NOTE: Avocado will oxidise (turns brown) when exposed to the air. A little lemon, lime juice or vinaigrette will avoid this.

GUACAMOLE

REFRIED BEANS

This recipe should be called TOMMY'S REFRIED BEANS… but I worried about nepotism. My son, Thomas, learned the basics from me. He made it so often that he developed his own flavour and some in the family would say better!

Makes enough for 4 to 6.

2 cups of cooked kidney beans – *drained and rinsed*
1 tin 330g of chopped tomatoes
1 big onion – *finely chopped*
2 cloves of garlic – *minced*
2 tbsp tomato paste

½ **tsp of chilli powder (pre-mixed)**
½ **tsp cumin seeds**
1 tsp ground cumin
1 tsp ground coriander
2 tbsp vegetable oil
1 tsp sea salt

1. Toast the cumin seeds in the dry pan for a minute.
2. Drop a little oil into the pan, once warm add the onion and the garlic.
3. When the onions are soft, add the chilli powder, ground cumin and ground coriander.
4. After another minute add the cooked kidney beans, the tomato paste and the juice from the tinned tomatoes.
5. Cook on a low heat for a good 5 minutes.
6. Mash the beans with your potato masher. Then add in the chopped tomatoes.
7. Allow all to reduce for 15 to 20 minutes.

Season with sea salt. Taste it; sometimes beans need a good bit of salt.

Perfect eaten with short grain brown rice, white rice or potatoes or put the pan in the middle of the table with a big pile of corn nachos and dig in!

These blank pages have been inserted with purpose; for your comments, other recipes, ideas... use them!

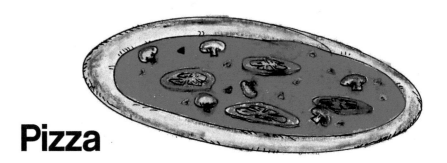

Pizza

When our children bring friends around for a little grub, it is the homemade pizza they prefer. Pizza is probably the world's most popular fast food and today, I could safely say, a college student's staple diet… after a night out!

Colm is our resident pizza connoisseur. He makes the dough and, while it is rising, he makes the sauce… his way! The student has almost surpassed the master… almost!

Here are a few ideas for toppings you might consider. But try your own; any leftover veggies, a drizzle of olive oil, a few chilli flakes, fresh chopped garlic… anything goes well on flat bread.

THE DOUGH

Makes 2 medium pizza bases.

3 cups strong wheat flour
1 packet fast acting dry yeast
1 cup warm water (not hot)
1 tsp sea salt
2 tbsp olive oil
½ tsp sugar

1. Mix the warm water, sugar and the yeast. Give it a few minutes; it should start to bubble, this means the yeast is active.
2. Add it to the flour with the oil. If too dry add a little water, if too wet add flour.
3. Form into a ball and knead it for 10 minutes, it should become springy.
4. Cover and allow to double in size, approx. 1 hour.
5. Add the salt and knead again for a minute.

This amount of dough will make 2 thick (1cm/½" thick) flat breads or 4 thin ones. You can roll out the dough very thin, 5mm/¼" or less, this will cook in minutes.

Once rolled, let it rest for 10 minutes before adding toppings and going into the oven.

THE SAUCE

Enough for 2 large pizzas.

1 tin of chopped tomatoes – *340ml*
2 tbsp tomato paste
1 or 2 garlic cloves – *minced*
1 tsp dried oregano
1 tbsp olive oil

1. Bring all together into a pot and allow to cook on a low heat.
2. Let it reduce for 15 minutes.
3. Use your potato masher to make the sauce a little smoother if you like it that way.

Allow to cool before using.

ZUCCHINI

This is quite a simple topping. I find that allowing one ingredient to dominate is perfect. Courgette and garlic is a perfect combination.

To cover 2 flat breads

1 courgette – *sliced into long thin strips*
1 garlic clove – *minced*
1 cup of tomato sauce
2 tbsp vegan cheeses (optional)

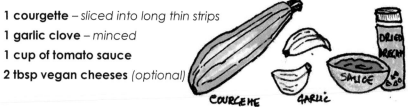

A little dried oregano
A light drizzle of olive oil

Have your oven hot, on at 220°C/500°F.

1. Quickly fry the courgette slices in a dry pan for a few minutes. While still hot cover with the garlic and olive oil. Set aside.
2. Roll out your dough as flat as you want it and place it onto the oven tray. Allow to rest for 10 minutes.
3. Cover with a layer of tomato sauce and insert in the bottom rack of your oven.
4. After 5 minutes, feel the bottom if it is a little firm take it out and place the strips of courgette over it.
5. You can add some vegan cheese if you like, but pizza tastes great without it as well.
6. Replace in the oven on the top rack and leave it for another 5 minutes… ready.

Sprinkle a little dried oregano over it as you take it out of the oven.

HOT & SPICY

There is nothing quite like flat bread with tomato sauce, a little lively chilli and garlic! Very simple but very tasty.

To cover 2 flat breads.

2 cloves of garlic – *finely chopped*
2 fresh tomatoes – *sliced in rounds*
1 cup of tomato sauce
Pinch of chilli flakes

Pinch of dried oregano
A drizzle of olive oil

Have your oven hot, on at 220°C/500°F.

1. Roll out your dough as flat as you want it, place it onto the oven tray and allow to rest for 10 minutes.
2. Spread a little sauce on the dough and place on the bottom rack in the oven.
3. After 5 minutes, check that the bottom is a bit firm.
4. Take it out of the oven and arrange the tomato slices all over the flat bread, sprinkle the garlic and the chilli flakes and drizzle a little olive oil over it.
5. Return it to the top rack of the oven for another 5 minutes.

Sprinkle a little dried oregano over it as you take it out of the oven.

L'AUBERGINE

Perhaps my favourite – aubergine/eggplant tastes great with just about anything. Combine it with tomato and olive oil and you have the wonderful flavour of the Mediterranean in your kitchen.

To cover 2 flat breads.

1 aubergine/eggplant – *sliced in thick rounds (1cm thick)*
1 fresh tomato – *finely chopped*
1 cup tomato sauce

1 tsp dried oregano
A drizzle of olive oil
Pinch of salt

Have your oven hot, on at 220°C/500°F.

1. Cut the aubergine in rounds 1cm thick (½"). Oil lightly a hot pan. Fry the aubergine on medium heat until brown. Turn over and brown other side. Check with a fork to make sure that they are soft inside, and set aside.
2. Roll out your dough as flat as you want it, place it onto the oven tray and allow to rest for 10 minutes.
3. Spread a little sauce on the dough and place on the bottom rack in the oven.
4. After 5 minutes check if bottom is a bit firm.
5. Take it out of the oven and arrange the slices of aubergine and chopped tomato and drizzle a little olive oil and a sprinkle of salt over it.
5. Return to the oven on the top shelf for another 5 minutes.

Sprinkle a little dried oregano over it as you take it out of the oven.

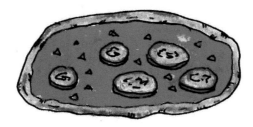

SWEET ONION

When onions are allowed to cook gently, they soften and sweeten to a most wonderful flavour. This is my version of the French onion flat bread called Pissaladiere. I was introduced to this from the cookbook *Sunshine Food* by Sophie Grigson.

To cover one large base.

3 red onions – *sliced into strips*
2 fresh tomatoes – *sliced into rounds*
10 black olives – *pitted and sliced in two*

½ tsp brown sugar
¼ cup red wine *(optional)*

Have your oven hot, on at 220°C/500°F.

1. Fry the sliced onions gently on a low heat until nearly soft, add the red wine and the sugar and simmer until all has come together nicely and any liquid has evaporated. Allow to cool.
2. Roll out your dough a little thicker, 1cm/½", and place it onto the oven tray. Allow to rest for 15 to 20 minutes.
3. Cover the dough with the onion 'sauce'.
4. Place the sliced tomatoes on top and sprinkle the olive halves between them.
5. Place on bottom shelf in the oven.
6. After 5 to 7 minutes, check that the bottom is firm.
7. Move the tray up to the top section and leave it another 5 to 7 minutes.

Serve hot or it's very nice cold as an appetiser or for brunch… well, anytime!

MUHAMMARA

Gatherings are about chatting, reminiscing or getting to know each other and at the heart of them is food and drink. At a reception at Saeid's home, we were treated to some interesting food and this is when I first tasted Muhammara on bread. I believe the origins are Syrian, but every country in the Middle East have their own version. This is mine!

To cover 2 flat breads.

2 sweet red peppers – *deseeded and halved*

1 onion – *finely chopped*

¼ cup of walnuts – *finely chopped*

1 cup of tomato sauce

2 cloves of garlic – *minced*

½ cup of breadcrumbs

1 tbsp lemon juice

1 tsp brown sugar

1 tsp chilli flakes

2 tbsp nutritional yeast

2 tbsp olive oil

A little sea salt

Get your oven hot, 220°C/500°F.

1. Put the pepper halves under a hot grill in the oven to blacken the skins. Allow to cool then remove the skin from the flesh, chop small and set aside.
2. Soften the onion and garlic in a little oil.
3. Mix together all the ingredients and fry for a few minutes so it all melts together, then set aside.
4. Roll out your dough thinly and place it onto the oven tray, allowing to rest for 5 minutes.
5. Spread a thin layer of Muhammara sauce over it and place in bottom section of the oven.
6. After 5 minutes check that the underside is a little firm.
7. Move the tray up to the top section and leave it another 5 minutes.

Sprinkle a little dried oregano and a drizzle of olive oil as you take it out.

These blank pages have been inserted with purpose; for your comments, other recipes, ideas... use them!

Main Course

When you are thinking of a big meal, these are the dishes. They are nearly enough all on their own but add potatoes or rice, maybe couscous, a salad or a few side dishes, and you have a feast. Served in smaller portions they make the perfect lunch.

NOTE: *This may look like a simple tin of kidney beans, but add to it a little spice, a few veggies and there is the potential to create some of the most tasty and filling of main courses!*

SATAY NOODLES

I first tasted satay (or Thai peanut) sauce while living in London. Sarah a flatmate from New Zealand made wonderful vegetarian dishes. Surfing the internet, I came across a recipe from Amanda* which was very similar, all those memories coming back to me.

Makes enough for 3.

250g linguine pasta
1 medium carrot – *grated*
¼ broccoli head – *broken into florets*
2cm/1" of fresh ginger – *minced*
1 garlic clove – *minced*
4 tbsp crunchy peanut butter

2 tbsp tamari or soy sauce
½ cup of water
1 tsp brown sugar
Pinch or two of chilli flakes
1 tbsp lime juice

1. In a small pot mix the ginger, the garlic, the lime juice and the tamari. Cook on a low heat for a minute then add the peanut butter and water. Mix well and set aside.
2. Bring a big pot of water to the boil and throw in the pasta. While the pasta is cooking, stir-fry the broccoli for a minute or two, just so it changes to a bright green colour. Set aside.
3. Once the pasta is al dente, strain off the water but keep a ½ cup.
4. To the hot pasta add the grated carrot and the broccoli and mix together.
5. Re-heat the satay sauce and pour over the pasta and the ½ cup of water. Mix well and serve immediately.

Serve with; *Crispy Tofu Cubes (p. 72) Cucumber Salad (p. 48).*

* *"Amanda's Thai Peanut" was the inspiration for this. Thank you, Amanda.*

BLACK BEAN BURGER

A night in, the feet up in front of the telly, a black bean burger with plenty of condiments, a large pile of home fries and a bottle of your favourite drink… a wonderful combination.

Makes enough for 4 to 6 burgers.

1 400g/16oz tin of black beans – *drained and rinsed*
1 green pepper – *deseeded and diced small*
1 onion – *finely chopped*
2 cloves of garlic – *minced*
1½ cups of breadcrumbs *(p. 24)*

½ tsp chilli flakes
1 tsp ground cumin
1 tbsp corn starch
Pinch of dried oregano
Sea salt and black pepp

1. Roughly mash the beans with a fork.
2. Add the corn starch, 1 cup of the breadcrumbs, the pepper, the onion and the garlic. If it seems a little too soft or wet add more breadcrumbs.
3. Shape two tablespoons of mixture into a burger shape, then coat with remaining bread crumbs and place them on the baking tray.
4. Cook in the oven at 180°C/360°F for 30 minutes, turn over and cook for another 15 minutes.
5. Allow to cool completely, they hold together better this way.
6. Re-heat in a frying pan for a few minutes.
7. Stuff into a good bread roll with spicy tomato sauce, lettuce, a little hummus, tomato slices, sweet onion slivers, dill pickle rounds… anything you might think of that seems good!

COLD BEER

Optional

I like to make a big batch, then freeze them – best fast food. Put one or as many as needed into your pan and heat gently for a few minutes, turning once to warm both sides and make sure they are well thawed out.

Serve with: *Plenty of home fries (p. 148) and garlic mayo (p. 113).*

CHICKPEA STEW

Dom, the older brother, lived in a small community. They often had parties where the food was 'pot luck', a tradition for gatherings where each person would bring a pot. This was his signature dish. He made it one day when I was visiting with my young wife. We have since adopted it as our own, of course with a few changes to avoid any copyright infringement.

Makes enough for 4 to 6 people.

2 tins of chickpeas – *drained and rinsed*
2 red peppers – *chopped small*
10 cloves of garlic – *coarsely chopped*
2 tins of chopped tomatoes

2 tsp of sweet paprika
A slick of olive oil
Sea salt

1. Heat a thin layer of olive oil in your large pot on a low heat and soften the peppers.
2. Add the garlic and cook for another few minutes, stirring from time to time so it does not burn.
3. Combine the chickpeas and the paprika and simmer for 5 minutes before adding the tomatoes.
4. Simmer with the lid half off for 30 minutes or until the juice from the tomatoes has nearly evaporated.

Serve with: *Short grain brown rice (p 152) Steamed veggies – broccoli or green beans, a green leaf salad (p 43).*

BIG CHILLI

There are some chefs who take their chilli very seriously, even keeping cooking methods and ingredients secret. Others cook it for hours allowing all the flavours to blend together; some like it mild and still others fiery hot. As with many of these slow cook dishes, the taste really comes out the next day and leftovers are nearly always better.

Makes enough for 4 to 6 people.

1 large onion – *finely chopped*

2 cloves of garlic – *minced*

2 green peppers – *chopped small*

1 large aubergine – *cubed small*

1 tin of chopped tomatoes

2 tins of pinto or kidney beans (4 cups)

2 tsp chilli powder*

½ tsp cumin seeds

A drop of vegetable oil

½ tsp dried oregano

1. Fry the onion and the cumin seeds on a low heat with a little oil.
2. After a few minutes add the garlic, the peppers and the aubergine and simmer until soft.
3. Sprinkle in all the spices and mix together.
4. Add the beans and the tomatoes and a pinch of oregano.
5. Let it cook slowly for 20 minutes or more.

Taste it and add a little salt at the end. You may like to make it spicier by adding more chilli, depending on your taste.

> NOTE: * The chilli powder I use is a blend of ground cumin, ground coriander, ground chilli and ground paprika.

TOFU BAKE

There is nothing kinder than to be invited to another's table. Our friends Sheila and Jim would often ring just as we were trying to decide what to cook for dinner. Our answer to their offer was always yes! Sheila made this dish and we took it as our own, a regular at the family table. Tofu is a fermented bean curd which needs a bit of marinating and some frying to give it flavour and texture.

Makes enough for 4 to 6.

1 block of firm tofu (400g) – drained *and* rinsed
1 cup of tomato sauce *(p. 110)*
½ courgette/zucchini – *sliced*
1 cup of mushrooms – *sliced*
A little chopped parsley/fresh herbs

Marinade:
¼ cup tamari (or soy sauce)
2 garlic cloves – *minced*
1 thumb's length of fresh ginger – *minced*

1. Slice the block of tofu into 10mm/½" thick slices.
2. Make the marinade and soak the tofu in it for a good hour, turning the slices regularly to get them well impregnated.
3. In a little oil fry each slice till they are lightly brown on both sides, set aside.
4. Slice the courgette and the mushrooms thinly, and sauté just enough to brown a little and bring out the taste.
5. On your baking tray lay out the tofu slices. Cover each piece with a layer of tomato sauce, and then place a few rounds of zucchini and mushrooms on each slice.
6. Heat the whole thing in the oven at 180°C/360°F for 20 minutes… sprinkle with chopped fresh herbs.

Serve with: *Hot mashed potato (p. 147) Steamed green beans (p. 126) Cabbage salad (p. 46).*

MINESTRONE

Minestrone is a chunky Italian soup known the world over. A tomato-based vegetable soup with beans, vegetables and a little pasta in a sweet broth infused with herbs – a complete meal in a pot. My friend Jim, a soup specialist (yes, the same one mentioned above, we are still eating at his table), said to me one day, "Soup is better after 4 days." I could not argue with him, I was devouring one of his wonderful creations.

Makes enough for 6 bowls.

1 leek – *washed and finely chopped* (you can also use an onion)

1 celery stick – *finely chopped*

2 garlic cloves – *sliced*

1 big carrot – *cubed*

1 zucchini/courgette – *cubed*

1 tin/2 cups of tomatoes – *roughly chopped*

3 tbsp tomato paste

1 tin/2 cups of white haricot beans or chickpeas

A handful of dry pasta – **small macaroni**

Water to cover it all

½ tsp dried mixed herbs or thyme

Drop of olive oil

Sea salt & black pepper

Serve with: *Big slices of French baguette or Italian bread.*

1. Soften the leek/onion, the celery and the garlic in a drop of olive oil, at low heat.
2. Add the chopped carrots.
3. A few minutes later add the courgette and the herbs.
4. Once the veggies are softening, perhaps after 2 minutes, add the tomatoes, the tomato paste, the beans and dried herbs.
5. Add enough water to cover it all.
6. Bring to the boil then add the pasta. Simmer for approx. 10 minutes until the pasta is al dente.
7. Taste it and add a little salt if required and a good grind of fresh black pepper.

BURRITOS

A burrito is a complete meal rolled up tight. A big bean wrap! Great to take with you if on the run or warmed in the oven and served on a plate with a few side dishes. It is a perfect meal when entertaining. They can be made ahead of time. Heat them in the oven while you prepare other parts.

Makes enough for 6.

3 cups refried beans – *page…*
1 red and 1 yellow pepper – *sliced*
1 zucchini/courgette – *sliced*
1 aubergine/eggplant – *cubed*
1 onion – *coarsely chopped*
6 soft large tortillas *(flour or corn)*
Sea salt

1. Prepare the refried beans and set aside.
2. Stir-fry the onion, the pepper and the courgette for only a few minutes; you want them a little crunchy.
3. Take a soft tortilla – flour or corn – and fill with 2 tbsp refried beans and some of the sautéed veggies and roll and fold it.
4. Place on a tray and warm them in an oven at 180°C for 15 to 20 minutes. The tortilla should be just starting to brown at the edges.

I find a tahini sauce over them to be very nice.

I have made the tahini sauce using a mixture of nut butters such as almond or cashew and the flavour was wonderful.

Serve with: *Fresh tomato salsa (p. 117) Guacamole (p. 79) Green leaf salad (p. 43) Short grain brown rice (p. 152) Tahini sauce (p. 116).*

RED LENTIL DHAL

Dhal means lentils. Red lentils make a wonderful creamy stew. Many years ago, while partaking of our dear friends', Bhagwant and Permjit's, hospitality, Carmel learnt how to make this traditional Indian dish. It has gone through several modifications, but this is the basic recipe and a staple dish on our table since.

Makes enough for 6.

1 ½ **cup of red lentils** – *rinsed*

1 **onion** – *finely chopped*

2 **cloves of garlic** – *minced*

1 **big carrot** – *bitesize pieces*

1 **red chilli** – *finely chopped*

A thumb's length of fresh ginger – *peeled*

1 **large tomato** – *chopped small*

1 **tsp cumin seeds**

½ **cup chopped coriander**

A drop of vegetable oil

Water

Sea salt – *to taste*

1. Rinse the lentils first then add to 3 times as much water as lentils.
2. Bring it to the boil and simmer until the lentils are soft, approx. 20 minutes. Cook uncovered.
3. At the 10-minute mark, add the carrots and ginger.
4. While the lentils are cooking, heat a little oil in a separate pan and fry the cumin seeds, the onion, the chilli pepper, and the garlic.
5. Once the onion is soft add the tomato and fry so all is melted together.
6. Add it to the cooked lentils and simmer for 10 to 15 minutes.

Lentils will need salt, so add a good tsp, you may even need more.

Serve with: *Pan-fired naan (p. 162) Green leaf salad (p. 43) Short grain brown rice (p. 152).*

LASAGNE

When I ask Anne Marie, the youngest of the family, what she would like for dinner, her first choice is always lasagne! She likes it very plain, or with the vegetables blended into the sauce. Carmel, on the other hand, prefers chunky vegetables and lots of them, so to please all, I often make two.

Makes enough for 6.

1 box of lasagne sheets
2 cups of tomato sauce *(p. 33)*
+ ½ cup of water mixed in with it
2 cups of cream sauce *(p. 34)*
Filling of choice ... see below
Oven proof casserole dish 30 x 20 cm

1. Cover the bottom of an oven proof dish with tomato sauce. Spread out a layer of the dried lasagne – break them if required to fit.
2. Spread more tomato sauce on the sheets, then a layer of filling and a layer of cream sauce.
3. Repeat this until you run out of filling, perhaps 3 or 4 layers.
4. On top of the last layer of pasta spread the last of the cream sauce.

Serve with: *Green leaf salad (p. 43) Crispy roast potatoes (p. 27) Garlic bread (see below)*

> *'Quick' Garlic Bread - Toast slices of French baquette or Italian bread, rub a glove of garlic over one side and drizzle with a little olive oil.*

Plain & Simple
Tomato sauce
Cream sauce

This is very plain, but everyone likes it, even cold. The tomato sauce and cream sauce work well between layers of pasta.

Mediterranean
1 aubergine
1 courgette / zucchini
1 sweet yellow pepper

Cube the aubergine, sprinkle a little salt over it and let it rest for 20 min. Squeeze out any juice. Heat a tbsp of oil and fry for a few minutes until soft. Cube the pepper and courgette and sweat them separately until soft. Mix together.

Sweet Onion
2 large sweet onions
A pinch of dried oregano

Cut the onion into large cubes and sweat on low heat until soft. Sprinkle a little dried oregano over the onions and use as a filling.

PUY LENTIL STEW

Growing up in a household with a French mother, lentils were regularly on the menu. The puy lentils originate from central France. We ate them in stews or cold as a salad with vinaigrette and plenty of fresh chopped parsley... of course. There is something very earthy and satisfying about lentils. A good bowl of warm lentils and one is content, if not happy.

Makes enough for 4.

1 cup of dried puy or green lentils – *rinsed*
1 onion – *finely chopped*
1 large carrot – *cut into bitesize pieces*
1 clove of garlic – *minced*
1 tomato – *chopped very small or mashed*
1 large potato – *cubed*

A drop of vegetable oil
1 lemon – *cut into 4 wedges to squeeze*
½ tsp of dried thyme

1. In your large pot fry the onion and the garlic on a low heat.
2. After a minute add the carrot, the potato and the thyme, cover and cook for a minute or two stirring from time to time.
3. Pour 3 cups of water into the pot and bring to the boil, then add the lentils, lower the heat and simmer until the lentils are almost soft.
4. Add the tomato at the end, and cook for another few minutes.

Serve with a wedge of lemon on the side for those who like it. The taste of lemon juice is wonderful with lentils.

Serve with: *Short grain brown rice (p. 152) Carrot salad (p. 44).*

FALAFEL

To make 'authentic' falafels you need a food processor or your trusty bullet blender. We are using dry chickpeas and they are very hard. Falafel are one of the most important foods in the Middle East. They are eaten as fast food in a bread pocket, on a plate in a sit-down restaurant and always at home.

Makes enough for 20 falafels – normally enough for 6 people.

2 cups of dry chickpeas (500g)

1 onion – *finely chopped*

3 cloves of garlic – *minced*

1 cup of breadcrumbs

2 tbsp flour

2 tbsp corn starch

1 to 2 cups of fresh parsley – *chopped up*

2 tbsp cumin powder

1 tsp sea salt

½ cup of vegetable oil – *for cooking*

1. Put the chickpeas in a pot of water, bring to the boil and cook for 10 minutes. Drain, allow to cool and use.
2. Prepare all the other ingredients and mix with the chickpeas.
3. Half fill your food processor and reduce the mixture, so the chickpeas are crumbly.
4. Make a ball with your hand: the mixture should hold together, if not, add a little water.
5. Heat the oil in your pan. Once hot drop in your falafel. After a minute, turn them so they brown all around.
6. Place on paper towel to remove some of the oil.

Falafel is often stuffed into pitta bread cut in half to create a pocket. Fill it with a little chopped lettuce or cabbage, slices of tomato and cucumber, hummus, tahini sauce and hot sauce.

Serve with: *Grated carrot and cabbage, Sliced tomatoes and cucumber, Slivers of sweet onion, Hummus (p. 78), Tahini sauce (p. 116), Hot sauce (p. 118).*

PEA & POTATO MASALA

I love Indian food in a restaurant. But homemade Indian food in the right hands is something to experience. So, eating at our friend Neelam's house is always a pleasure. Neelam served something like this when we once visited her. My children, who never eat Indian food, devoured it. I try recreating it for them, but I am often reminded that, "… it is good, but not like Neelam's."

Makes enough for 4 to 6 people.

2 potatoes – *peeled & cubed*

1 cup green peas – *frozen*

1 onion – *finely chopped*

2 garlic cloves – *peeled & sliced*

1 tsp cumin seeds – *ground*

¼ tsp turmeric powder

1 tbsp tomato paste

A drop of vegetable oil

½ tsp chili flakes

1 tbsp Fresh cilantro

A tsp of lemon juice

1. In your pot soften the onion, garlic and cumin seeds in the drop of oil.
2. Add the tomato paste, the chilli flakes and the turmeric.
3. Add 2 cups of water and the cubed potatoes.
4. Bring to the boil and cook covered for 5 minutes then add the peas and cook for another 5 minutes or until the potatoes are cooked.
5. Season with salt and pepper, a ½ tsp of lemon juice and the cilantro leaves. Taste it, you may need a little more.

I serve this with stove top, pan fried 'Naan' bread, not the traditional way, but it works and no one complains (p. 162).

FUL MEDAMES... *Syrian beans mix*

Muhammad, my Syrian friend, made this for me when I was visiting him in Canada; a great cook! The recipe was originally from Damascus, the source of much great food, I was informed. I did not argue; the food was delicious.

Makes enough for 4 as a midday meal.

1 tin of chickpeas, 400g *– drained and rinsed*
2 tins of fava beans, 800g *– drained and rinsed*
(if fava beans unavailable use other beans)
2 garlic cloves *– sliced*
2 large tomatoes *– cubed*
½ cup fresh parsley *– finely chopped*
½ tsp ground cumin

Drizzle of olive oil
2 green onions *– whole*
A cup of hummus
4 pitta breads
Juice of ½ a lemon
2 wedges of lemon per person
Sea salt

1. Drain and rinse the chickpeas and the fava beans.
2. In your pot combine the chickpeas, fava beans, the garlic and cover with water. Bring to the boil then immediately drain off the liquid. Allow to cool.
3. Put the cooled fava beans and chickpeas in a large serving dish, sprinkle with a good pinch of salt then cover with the chopped tomatoes and the parsley, the juice of half a lemon and a good drizzle of olive oil.

Serve with a small plate of hummus each, the green onions, the lemon wedges and warm pita bread, with plenty of Middle Eastern tea.

ROASTED VEGGIE SQUARES

Carmel came home after having lunch at a friend's house. As it happens an amateur gourmet was in attendance and she made these tasty squares. The description started my mouth watering. I immediately tried to copy it and this is how it turned out. It has very French overtones so it all came naturally to me... bien sur!

Makes enough for 4 people.

1 frozen puff pastry sheet – *thawed*
1 sweet red pepper – *cubed*
1 courgette – *cubed*
½ small aubergine – *cubed*
1 onion – *cut into small chunks*

2 garlic cloves – *peeled & whole*
2 tbsp olive oil
4 tbsp vegan cream cheese

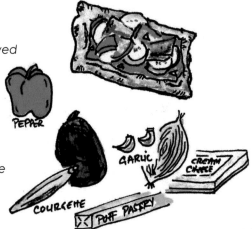

1. Take the frozen puff pastry out of the freezer an hour or so before cooking.
2. Put all the veggies on a tray into the oven at 180°C for 20 minutes. Once they have softened a little take them out. Drizzle a little olive oil over them, sprinkle with sea salt, mix well.
3. Lay out a thawed sheet of puff pastry and cut into four. Spoon enough of the roasted veggies onto the square pastry allowing a boarder of 2cm/1" all around.
4. Drop a thin spoon or two of vegan cheese on each square.
5. Place in the oven for 20 minutes or until the edges of the pastry are browning.

Serve with:
boiled new potatoes and cherry tomato and garlic sauce (p.109).

These blank pages have been inserted with purpose; for your comments, other recipes, ideas... use them!

La Sauce

A meal can depend so much on the sauce. Simple boiled potatoes and a warm sauce can be a dish, almost a meal, especially if it is fresh chopped garlic, a sprinkle of salt and a good drizzle of olive oil!

Sauce can come in many forms. Very plain or an elaborate hearty tomato and red pepper sauce with mixed vegetables and beans, it just needs to be somewhat wet and runny.

CHERRY TOMATO & GARLIC

The combination of the small tomatoes cooked in their skins, the garlic and the olive oil creates a sweet umami* flavour. These need to be cooked on a low heat slowly. For Pasta, Pizza, New Potatoes, Any Savoury Pastry Dish.

Enough to share between 4 or 6.

2 handfuls of cherry tomatoes *– whole*
5 to 10 cloves of garlic *– peeled & whole*

¼ cup of extra virgin olive oil
Fresh basil *(if available)*
Pinch of sea salt

1. In a pot drop in the cherry tomatoes whole. Peel the garlic but leave the cloves whole. Turn up the heat. When you hear a sizzle turn it down very low, pour in the olive oil and a pinch of salt and stir well.
2. Cook uncovered for 20 minutes or until the tomatoes have begun to melt.
3. Rip up the leaves of basil and sprinkle on top as you serve.

> NOTE: *Umami – Japanese term that we now consider a fifth flavour: savoury flavour. Was always there, we now just have a cool name for it!*

CLASSIC TOMATO

This sauce will go with just about anything, if it is a tomato sauce you want. You can add a number of other veggies to give it more body and texture – peppers, aubergine, even kidney beans. For Pasta & Pizza.

Makes about enough for two with pasta; if you add more veggies you may be able to serve 4.

1 tin of chopped tomatoes
1 onion – *finely chopped*
½ a carrot – *grated*
½ a small courgette – *grated*
1 clove of garlic – *minced*

Pinch of dried oregano
A drop of olive oil
Pinch of salt
A grind of black pepper

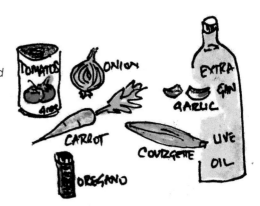

1. Heat a drop of olive oil in your pot on low heat and add the onion. After a minute add the garlic.
2. Give it another minute then add the carrot and the courgette.
3. Once all starts to soften throw in the tin of tomatoes and a pinch of dried oregano.
4. Simmer for 10 minutes, done!
5. Add salt and a nice bit of ground black pepper.

ONION GRAVY

Onion gravy is pure umami, a wonderful savoury taste. Slow cooked with just a little thickener, the onion becomes rich and strong tasting. For Savoury Pastry Dishes, Potatoes & Nut Roasts.

Makes about 2 ½ cups of gravy, enough for 4 to 6 servings.

1 onion – finely chopped
1 garlic clove – minced
2 tbsp olive oil
3 tbsp flour
2 cups water

1 tbsp tamari or soy sauce
Ground black pepper
Pinch of salt to taste

1. Heat the olive oil and soften the onion and the garlic.
2. Sprinkle the flour over the onions, add a tablespoon of the water and mix well so there are no lumps.
3. Add the rest of the water and the tamari and bring to the boil, stirring continuously until all starts to thicken.
4. Turn off the heat and season with a grind of black pepper. Taste it to see if it needs a little salt. Tamari is quite salty, you may not need any more.

CREAMY WHITE SAUCE

This is a very easy cream sauce to make and it works every time… if you follow the instructions, of course. You will use it with lasagne, with pasta bakes, or even over steamed vegetables. For Lasagne & Macaroni Bakes.

Makes about 2 ½ cups of gravy.

2 tbsp of whole wheat flour
2 tbsp margarine
2 cups of almond or soya milk
1 garlic clove – *minced*
½ onion – *finely chopped*
¼ cup butter beans – *mashed* (optional)

1 tsp of Dijon mustard
1 tbsp nutritional yeast
1 tsp of sea salt at the end
1 tbsp olive oil

1. Melt the margarine, add the flour and mix so all oil is absorbed. This is called a 'roux' by French chefs. You can brown it slightly to give it a stronger taste.
2. Slowly add the nut, milk stirring continuously so the roux melts into the milk without any lumps* then bring it to the boil and simmer, mixing until it starts to thicken. Set aside.
3. Warm the oil on a low heat in the pot and soften the onion and garlic together. If using butter beans, add them now. With your potato masher or a fork mash into a paste. (You can also blend this to make it very smooth.)
4. Add the mash to the sauce with the Dijon and the nutritional yeast. Taste it for salt.

---

* Avoiding lumps is the only difficult part of making the cream sauce.
Troubleshooting:
- *Accept the sauce with a few lumps, get over it.*
- *Put roux & milk in blender first, then heat slowly and stir continuously.*
- *Be very careful to add only a little liquid at a time, stirring continuously. It may take a little practice. I find a whisk helps.*

VEGAN MAYO

I had been trying to make my own veggie mayo with various different ingredients. Spending some time at the wonderful vegetarian restaurant in Dublin, Cornucopia, I was introduced by the chef, Lily, to a very tasty mayo used in their potato salad. My addition was garlic – la piece de resistance? Of course, this is only a matter of taste. For Sandwiches, French Fries, Salads.

Makes approx. 1 ½ cups of mayo.

1 cup vegetable oil (not olive oil)*
½ cup soya milk
2 tbsp apple cider vinegar
1 tbsp Dijon mustard

1 garlic clove – *minced* (optional)
Pinch of sea salt

1. In a deep bowl combine the soya milk, the cider vinegar, the Dijon, the garlic and the salt. Use an immersion blender, regular blender or food processor.
2. Blitz this a few times until smooth.
3. Slowly add the oil a little at time while blending. With each amount added, make sure it is well mixed in before adding more.
4. After a time it will start to thicken. If it does not, add a little more oil until it does.

Transfer to a glass jar and refrigerate.

> ** Olive oil is strong; it can be used of course, but the lighter vegetable oil gives the mayo a more neutral taste. You can add a little olive oil at the end for taste.*

SATAY PEANUT SAUCE

This sauce is one that surprises me every time I make it. Such a wonderful flavour and I never make enough of it! Steam a few vegetables – an onion quartered, a big carrot, some turnip, a few baby potatoes. Once cooked, pour this sauce over them, a wonderful meal! For Pasta, Boiled Veggies, Noodles, Tofu.

Makes enough to cover vegetables for 4 servings.

4 tbsp crunchy peanut butter
Thumb-length piece of fresh ginger *– minced*
1 garlic clove *– minced*
1 shallot *– finely chopped*
1 red chilli *– minced*
½ cup of shredded coconut (optional)

1 tbsp lime juice
1 tbsp maple syrup or other sweetener
1 tbsp tamari (or 2 of soy sauce)
1 tbsp vegetable oil
1 cup water
A pinch of sea salt

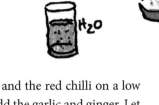

1. In a saucepan fry the shallot and the red chilli on a low heat. After a minute or two add the garlic and ginger. Let it all soften a minute more.
2. Add the 4 tbsp of crunchy peanut butter, the ½ a cup of water (a little more if you want it runny), the tamari and the shredded coconut.
3. Simmer on a low heat for 5 minutes.
4. At the end add the lemon juice and maybe a pinch of salt, taste it.

SWEET & SOUR

If you are making stir-fry on a regular basis, double or triple the recipe and keep in the fridge, otherwise make this before you start cooking. Sometimes starch is used which mimics store bought-sauce. I prefer the sauce runny and lighter. For Stir Fry.

Makes enough to cover vegetables for 4 servings.

¼ cup of tamari soy sauce

Thumb-length piece of fresh ginger *– minced*

1 garlic clove *– minced*

½ small red chilli – *minced (seeds removed)*

2 tbsp maple syrup or other sweetener

3 tbsp cider vinegar

¼ cup of water

1. Prepare all the ingredients and mix together.
2. Ready!

TAHINI SAUCE

Sesame seed butter sauce is a staple in much of the desert population of the Middle East, made from what is found locally. For Falafel & Burritos.

½ cup tahini – *sesame butter*
3 garlic cloves – *minced*
½ cup water
¼ cup lemon juice
Pinch of sea salt

1. Combine all the ingredients.
2. Mix well.
3. Ready.

If you have a bullet blender pour everything into it and blend smooth.
    Keeps in the refrigerator for a few weeks.

FRESH SALSA

When you make bean dishes, especially wraps, it is nice to have something juicy and fresh to accompany them. The fresh coriander makes it even livelier. Wonderful eaten with a big bowl of corn chips. For Burritos, Nachos.

Makes sauce to serve 4 burritos.

10+ cherry tomatoes – *quartered or minced*
½ red onion – *finely chopped*
1 or 2 garlic cloves – *minced*

Juice of 1 lemon
2 tbsp coriander or parsley – *finely chopped*
2 tbsp olive oil
Pinch of salt

1. Mix all the ingredients together.
2. Let it sit in the fridge for 15 minutes or so to allow the flavours to come together well.

Make this fresh; the next day it is never the same.

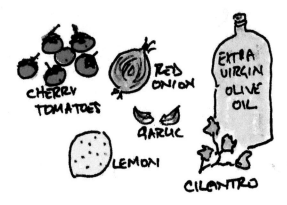

HOT SAUCE

Hot sauce you always need to have on hand. When cooking there may be those individuals who do not like their food too spicy. In that case it is courteous to cook without chilli and have sauce on the side or on the table for people to add it themselves. For Falafel, Burgers, Burritos, Sandwiches, Pasta... Anything!

Makes about enough to have for a few meals. Store in glass jar in the fridge.

4 small hot chilli peppers – *finely chopped, seeds included*
(or 4 tsp chilli flakes)
½ onion – *finely chopped*
4 tbsp tomato paste
¼ cup of water
¼ cup apple cider vinegar
2 cloves of garlic – *minced*
½ tsp of sugar

A drop of olive oil
Pinch of salt

1. Heat a drop of olive oil in your pot on a low heat and add the onion. After a minute add the garlic and a pinch of salt.
2. Give it another minute then add the chilli.
3. Once all starts to soften, add to the blender with the tomato paste, the sugar, the salt, the vinegar and the water.
4. Blend it together so it is very smooth.

NOTE: HOT SAUCE
How hot the sauce is will depend on the chilli you use.
If you want it milder, take out the seeds and it
will still have a nice taste.

These blank pages have been inserted with purpose; for your comments, other recipes, ideas... use them!

On The Side

To me a meal is most interesting when there are 4 or 5 parts to it. Side dishes are normally accompaniments to the main course, but some can be good as starters and you can even make a meal by combining several of them together.

There is always someone who does not like spicy food, or coriander, or garlic (what!!? Yes, these people do exist), so variety in a meal is good.

CHICKPEAS & CUMIN

Carmel started making something similar to this dish and the young and now not-so-young ones in the family really liked it. I added the smoked paprika because the college student 'children' are addicted to it: my part, my book! Perfect with mashed potatoes.

Makes enough for 4.

1 tin of chickpeas – *drained and rinsed*
2 cloves of garlic – *minced*
½ an onion – *finely chopped*

½ tsp cumin seeds
½ tsp ground cumin
Drop of vegetable oil
¼ tsp smoked paprika
Sea salt

1. Toast the cumin seeds on a low heat in your dry pan for a minute.
2. Add a drop of oil, the onion and garlic and soften gently.
3. Mix in the ground cumin, the smoked paprika and finally the chickpeas.
4. Cook on a low heat, stirring from time to time until all has combined well with the chickpeas.
5. Taste and add a little salt if required.

They can also be made as **finger food** for a gathering – once the cooking is done, spread the chickpeas on your tray and place in the oven at 180°C to dry out for 10 to 15 minutes. Sprinkle a little ground cumin on them as they come out of the oven. Allow to cool before serving.

CREAMED SPINACH

I brought this for a party, a pot luck gathering of friends. Their adolescent son, Rory, appreciated it. I had not considered including it here, but the encouragement from this young man was all I needed. Rory has asked me on more than one occasion when this collection of recipes will ever be published, so here it is, finally!

Makes enough for 4.

Big bunch of fresh spinach, 250g – *washed*
(baby spinach if available)
1 onion – *finely chopped*
1 clove of garlic – *minced*
¼ tsp cumin seeds
½ tsp ground cumin
Drop of vegetable oil
Pinch (¼ tsp) of turmeric
Pinch of sea salt

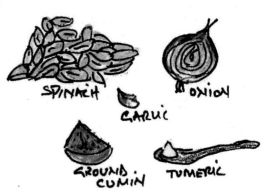

1. If you are using big leaves cut out the large centre stem and tear up the leaves into smaller pieces. If you can get baby spinach, all the better as it melts to a lovely smooth texture.
2. Put the washed, but not dried, spinach into a pot on a low heat. Stir occasionally as it melts. This takes only a few minutes. Do not overcook or it will lose its colour and taste. Set aside.
3. Fry the onion, garlic and cumin seeds gently in a little oil for a minute until soft then add the ground cumin and the turmeric. After a few minutes add the spinach and stir until you get a smooth paste. You may need to add a little water if it is too dry.
4. Season with a little salt at the end.

If you have a food processor, it can be reduced to a very smooth texture.

FRIED ONIONS

Many recipes start with frying onions, they add such wonderful flavour. So why not make fried onions on their own to serve as a side dish? Wonderful with any potato dish and as a condiment for burgers. Cut them the long way, in 5mm strips, not too small and cook them very slowly.

Makes enough for 4 servings.

2 onions – *cut in strips*

A pinch of dried oregano,
… or sage, or a sprig of rosemary
A drop of vegetable oil
¼ tsp chilli flakes (optional)
Pinch of sea salt

1. Fry the onion in a little oil on a very low heat, and sprinkle a little sea salt on top, mixing once or twice so they do not stick to the pan.
2. When they are soft, sprinkle a little oregano over them and mix well.

The other day I added a ¼ tsp of chilli flakes, wow…

CHILLI ONIONS!

BABY SPUDS & VINAIGRETTE

Another way to serve potatoes – to me, any way is a good way, but this is perfect when the new season potatoes become available. A warm 'salad'.

Makes enough for 4.

10 baby new potatoes *– washed*
1 clove of garlic *– minced*
One or two spring onions *– finely chopped*

Fresh parsley *– finely chopped*
2 tbsp vinaigrette
Pinch of salt
Grind of black pepper

1. Boil, or even, better steam the baby potatoes until soft, then drain.
2. While still hot, cut the potatoes in two and place in your big bowl.
3. Add the garlic and the spring onion to the warm potatoes and mix together. Allow to sit for a few minutes for the garlic and onion to soften in the heat.
4. Mix in the parsley, the vinaigrette and a good pinch of salt and black pepper to taste.

GARLIC MUSHROOMS

We sat at our friends', Malachi and Evelyn's, table and the meal included these garlic mushrooms. When I complimented the wonderful taste, I was told they were their son Donal's recipe. And there was a story associated with the recipe, something to do with bribing a rugby team from down under with food for a signed football. We all know that good food will get you anything you want…

Makes enough for 4.

2 handfuls of mushrooms – *cut in 4*
2 cloves of garlic – *roughly chopped*

Lots of fresh parsley – *finely chopped*
Sea salt
Black pepper

1. Rinse the mushrooms under the tap, do not bother to dry.
2. Quarter them.
3. Heat the pan on a medium heat. Toss in the mushrooms and stir for a minute until almost dry.
4. Add the garlic and cook for another minute or two, but no longer or the garlic will burn.
5. Take it off the heat, sprinkle a little salt and good ground black pepper over it all.
6. I like to add a nice handful of chopped fresh parsley. Mix well and serve.

The key is not to overcook the mushrooms, you want a lively flavour.

FRENCH GREEN BEANS

Growing up, the whole family helped in our kitchen. We each had our specialities. My father's job was to nip the ends of the green beans and snap them. He would sit at the table and converse, his favourite pastime, all the while snapping the long green bean into smaller bitesize pieces. Green beans were a staple of the French household.

Makes enough for 4.

1 handful of green beans, 150g – *washed & trimmed*
2 cloves of garlic – *sliced*

Fresh parsley
Sea salt

1. Trim the ends of the beans and keep them long.
2. Steam the beans in a thin layer of water on a low to medium heat for about 5 minutes, stirring so they do not burn.
3. When you feel that the beans are about to soften but are still a little firm – check one with your teeth – add the garlic and cook for another minute. At the end add the parsley and a sprinkle of salt.

Cover and allow to stand for a minute before serving.

SAUCY KIDNEY BEANS

Sometimes you need something hearty, something fast to complete the meal and this is it. Kidney beans, soft onions, a little salt, and a hint of cumin. Of course, if you have a red pepper chop it up and add to the onions. An additional wonderful flavour.

Makes enough for 4.

1 tin of kidney beans – *drained, rinsed*
1 onion – *finely chopped*
1 clove of garlic – *minced*

½ tsp cumin seeds
Drop of vegetable oil
Sea salt
Black pepper

1. Heat a dry pan on a low heat, toss in the cumin seeds and toast for 30 seconds to bring out the flavour.
2. Add a drop of olive oil and soften the onion and garlic gently.
3. Drain the can of kidney beans, rinse and add to the onions. Cook gently for 10 minutes or so.

Taste it, it may need a pinch of salt and a grind of black pepper. With canned beans, better to rinse them well.

N.B.
If you cook your own beans keep the liquid, it has a lot of the nutrients. Perfect for soups, or to make a stew with.

MEDITERRANEAN BUTTER BEANS

When spending time at our local market looking for fresh marinated olives, I came across these butter beans. I had to try and make them myself! Butter beans are mild and go well with the addition of strong herbs or spices. If you can make this a day before, all the flavours will blend together. Perfect for a brunch.

Makes enough for 4 people

1 tin of butter beans – *drained & rinsed*
2 scallions/spring onions – *finely chopped*
2 or 3 sun-dried tomatoes – *coarsely chopped*
2 garlic cloves – *minced*

A pinch of chilli flakes
4 tbsp olive oil
Pinch of sea salt

1. Drain and rinse the butter beans. In a pot cover the beans with a little water and bring to the boil, then drain the water.
2. Add all the other ingredients while the beans are still hot and mix well.
3. Allow to marinate for 20 minutes before serving. If you make this the day before, the taste is even better; refrigerate overnight.

Taste it, you may like a little more salt.

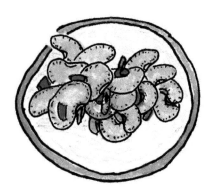

COLCANNON

Irish traditional mashed potatoes. Plain mashed potato tastes great, but there is a version in Ireland which turns this simple side dish into something hearty and substantial. A few fried onions for flavour and plenty of soft cabbage or kale.

Makes enough for 6.

6 big potatoes – *washed & quartered*
2 onions – *cut into strips*
2 cups curly kale or
cabbage – *chopped in strips*
Sea salt
Black pepper
2 tbsp olive oil

1. Put the potatoes in a big pot, cover half with water, bring to the boil and simmer until soft, 10 to 15 minutes should do it. Drain and keep the water.
2. Sprinkle the onion with a little salt and fry in a drop of olive oil on a low heat until soft. Set aside.
3. Wash the kale and cut into strips, removing the heavy stem. Cook the kale separately in a pot with a sprinkle of water until wilted.
4. Mash the potatoes well, add a little of the water if too dry and a good sprinkle of salt and the olive oil.
5. Mix together with the onions and kale… and serve piping hot.

Taste it; add salt if required.

STUFFED MUSHROOMS

These you can use as a starter dish, three or four on the plate, as appetisers put out to have with the drinks as your guests arrive or a few as a side dish – perfect with mashed potatoes.

Makes enough for 6 people.

20 small (mouthful size) mushrooms – *stems removed*

Stuffing:
1 tomato – *seeds removed & finely chopped*
The stems – *finely chopped*
1 cup of breadcrumbs
½ cup ground almonds
1 clove of garlic – *minced*
½ cup of fresh parsley – *finely chopped*
(dried oregano is nice as well)

A drizzle of olive oil
A grind of black pepper

1. Mix all ingredients for the filling together.
2. Using a spoon, fill each mushroom cap with a rounded mount, pressing well to pack in the filling.
3. Place on a tray and into a hot oven (200°C/400°F) for 10 minutes.

Allow to cool a bit before serving.

These blank pages have been inserted with purpose; for your comments, other recipes, ideas... use them!

Sweet Thing

I generally do not eat dessert after dinner, though it is the custom for many. To me it takes away the great savoury taste from the meal and I like it to linger... especially if it is garlic! Better to wait half an hour or more, allowing the meal to digest before the sweet thing.

I have read that eating sweet food after eating savoury has an adverse effect on digestion – sugar and good digestion do not mix. From experience I have found that eating dessert after a big meal is not the best. But there is nothing like a few sweet snacks in the afternoon... a wonderful Spanish custom.

FRUIT SALAD

This has been handed down from our French tradition through the family via my mother, from her mother and her mother before that. I have watched my mother make it for years, actually I have been 'encouraged' to help her on many occasions. Vibrant colours and pure freshness!

Makes enough for 4 to 6.

2 apples – *washed, cored & cut small*

1 pears – *washed, cored & cut small*

2 kiwis – *peeled and cut small*

1 banana – *peeled and cut in rounds*

4 oranges – *for juice*

1. Cut the oranges in two, make juice using a lemon squeezer and put it into a large bowl. Orange juice from the shop is completely different; a different taste and tanginess.
2. I like to cut the fruit up small and of similar size, but it is really a matter of taste.
3. Mix all well and let it stand in the fridge for 20 minutes before serving.

Very nice served alone or with light biscuits or light sponge cake.

Any combination of fruit is good. If you can get pineapple or mango they give it a tropical flavour. A mixture of berries can be very nice – strawberries, blueberries, raspberries and even grapes, but better cut in two… thanks Jim.

APPLE CRUMBLE

Apple crumble is one of those desserts that looks very good, tastes great and is so easy to make… win, win, win – from the modern vernacular.

Can be shared by 6 to 8 people, but I often prefer 4!

4 large cooking apples – *peeled, cored and cut into chunks.*
1 cup of flour
½ cup of oats
¼ cup of nuts: walnuts or pecans – *chopped up*
½ cup of brown sugar
½ cup of vegetable butter

1. Mix the chunks of apple with 2 tbsp of the sugar, making sure they are well coated.
2. Cover the bottom of a greased baking tray with the apples.
3. Mix together the flour and the rest of the sugar, then add the butter, rubbing together with your fingers until well blended.
4. Mix the oats and chopped nuts into the flour.
5. Sprinkle the mixture evenly over the apples.
6. Put into a preheated oven at 190°C/375°F/gas mark 5 for approx. 30 minutes… or until the top is nice and brown!

APPLE TART

I never ate good apple tart until I met Peggy, my future mother-in-law. She did not know it at the time and neither did I, but the tarts may have helped! I had eaten apple pie before, but it was never like hers. The right amount of pastry to fruit and the right amount of sweetness, actually slightly tart! Apple tart… makes sense!

A tart this size can be shared by 6 to 8 people – Peggy's, better only by 4!

4 large cooking apples – *peeled, cored and sliced*
3–4 tbsp sugar
Short crust pastry *(p. 165)*

2 cups/250 g plain flour
2/3 cup of vegetable margarine
4 to 5 tbsp cold water

1. Put the flour in your big bowl and add the margarine. Cut in with a butter knife as small as possible, then use your hands to make it crumbly… but quickly, you do not want to warm the mixture.
2. Add the cold water one spoon at a time until you can form the pastry dough.
3. Refrigerate for 20 minutes before rolling out on a well-floured surface.
4. Roll out half the pastry and cover the bottom of a well-greased pie plate. Spread the apple slices evenly on the pastry and sprinkle the sugar on top.
5. Roll out the second half of the pastry and cover the apples, crimping the edges with a fork and piercing the top to allow the steam out or it might burst.
6. Put into a preheated oven at 190°C/375°F/gas mark 5 for approx. 30 minutes… or until the top is nice and brown!

STEWED FRUIT

Dawn, my cousin from London, has stewed fruit on her stove top nearly every day – her staple. She serves it with everything: cake, tart, crumble. If there is nothing available, she eats it on its own. Spending time with her gave me the taste for it. I find this sauce gives sweet sponge cake a little added moisture and a wonderful tartness!

Makes enough for 4 with cake or 1 if you are indulging yourself and only want to eat the fruit stew.

2 handfuls of raspberries blueberries or strawberries, or a mixture of them all.
4 or 5 plums – *stones taken out then chopped*
¼ cup of water
½ tsp of sugar
Drop of brandy (optional... but why not?)

1. Put all the ingredients together in your pot on a low heat and slowly melt the fruit.
2. Stir from time to time so it cooks evenly. This should take 15 to 20 minutes.
3. Taste. It may be a little too sour; add ½ tsp of sugar if required, but go light with the sugar – you want to keep the fresh tart fruit flavour, it needs to contrast with the sweet cake (see next page!).

N.B. If you choose to add the brandy, the alcohol evaporates with cooking, but the flavour remains.

BERRIES   PLUMS   WATER

SUGAR

SPONGE CAKE

A simple golden-coloured sponge cake that is good for any occasion. Icing sugar can be powdered over it (when cool) to give it a little colour… 'snow' topped. It is also perfect in combination with the tarty stewed fruit sauce.

Makes one medium sized cake.

1½ cups plain flour
1 cup of granulated sugar
1 tsp baking powder

¼ cup vegetable oil
1 tbsp apple cider vinegar
1 cup of nut milk or water
2 tsp vanilla essence

1. Mix all the dry ingredients together in a bowl.
2. Mix the wet ones separately then add to the dry mixture.
3. Mix well so everything is well blended.
4. Grease a rectangular or round tin, 25cm/9x9 inches in size. Line the bottom with greaseproof paper.
5. Pour the mixture into the tin and even it out.
6. Bake for 30 minutes or until a cocktail stick inserted into the middle of the cake comes out clean.
7. Cool for 10 minutes, turn over so it comes out of the tin and allow to cool before serving.
8. Preheat oven to 190ºC/375ºF/gas mark 5.

CHOCOLATE CAKE

The classic – we all need a chocolate cake even if it is only for birthdays. But why not when you feel like it?! This one is so easy. Put it together in fifteen minutes, ready in less than an hour.

Makes one layer 2cm/1 inch.
Double recipe for a birthday cake and stick the two pieces together with a layer of icing.

1½ cups of plain flour
1 cup granulated sugar
1 tsp baking powder
3 tbsp good cocoa powder

1 cup of nut milk: almond or soya
1 tsp apple cider vinegar
1 tsp vanilla
½ tsp salt
¼ cup of vegetable oil

Get your oven up to 180°C/350°F.

1. Mix all the dry ingredients together in a bowl.
2. Mix the wet ones separately then add to the dry mixture.
3. Mix well so everything is well blended.
4. Grease a 20cm/9x9" cake tin, lined with greaseproof paper so you can get it out.
5. Pour the mixture into the tin and even it out.
6. Bake for approx. 35 min.

Check after 30 minutes with a toothpick and if it comes out clean it is ready.

THE ICING

When you are making the cake for a birthday you want to make it special and icing is necessary. Emma, the 'dessert chef' when in residence, helped me master this.

Makes enough for one cake.

½ **cup icing sugar**
4 tbsp margarine
2 tbsp almond/soy milk
100g dark chocolate – *melted*
2 tbsp peanut butter
Pinch of salt
2 tsp vanilla extract

1. Melt the bar of chocolate, allow to cool a minute.
2. In your big bowl, put everything but the icing sugar together and mix until smooth, including the melted chocolate.
3. Sift in the icing sugar at the end. Use a whisk or your blender/food processor.
4. Allow to set for 20 minutes or more.
5. Spread it on your cake.

PEANUT BUTTER COOKIES

There is nothing better than a big batch of homemade peanut butter cookies in your cupboard when you get home and are hungry. Very good to help with the homework! I had been trying to come up with a good recipe when my cousin Casey, from Canada, happened to be staying with us. She told us that this was a fool-proof recipe. Of course, I had to make a few small changes but thanks to her we have this.

Makes 30 medium cookies.

1 cup vegetable margarine
1 cup dark brown sugar
1 cup white sugar
1 cup crunchy peanut butter – *only peanuts*
¼ cup of water
1 tsp pure vanilla extract

3 cups whole wheat flour
2 tsp baking powder
½ tsp sea salt

1. Blend well the margarine and sugar until the sugar melts into the fat.
2. Add the vanilla water and the peanut butter.
3. Put together the flour, the baking powder and the salt.
4. Add the dry ingredients bit by bit, making sure all is blended into a soft dough.
5. Drop rounded tablespoons full onto your greased tray, then press them down with a fork.
6. Place on middle shelf. The cooking time is only about 10 minutes. Check that they are slightly brown underneath. They come out soft but will harden upon cooling.
7. Pre-heat oven at 180°C/350°F.

NOTE: *The peanut butter that you use will make a big difference to the taste – best to use a type that only has peanuts in and nothing else.*

CHOCOLATE-COVERED DATES

I dropped into my sister Mairead's house to avail of a fine cup of coffee. She produced these wonderful chocolate dates. I had to ask how she made them in order to slip them into the book! They were actually made by her daughter, my niece! The next generation gives us much hope!

Makes enough for 6 people.

24 medjool dates – other types will work

24 almonds – **unsalted & roasted**

2 100g bars of dark chocolate – broken up

1 tsp vegetable butter

¼ tsp of vanilla extract

¼ cup roasted nuts – finely chopped almonds or pistachio

1. Cut the dates down the middle and remove the stones.
2. Insert a roasted almond in its place and squeeze shut.
3. In a pot on a very low heat, melt the vegetable butter and the chocolate. When runny mix in the vanilla.
4. Dip each date into the chocolate, making sure it is well covered, and set on a tray.
5. Sprinkle a little of the chopped nuts on each.
6. Refrigerate until the chocolate has hardened.

Take the dates out of the fridge 10 to 15 minutes before serving.

COCONUT SQUARES

Aveen is Mairead's daughter, my niece, the one who made the chocolate covered dates. She also made these, she makes a lot of things with chocolate, we are all blessed. These are in a different category to normal dessert; one might say pure decadence.

Makes enough for 6 people.

3 cups of shredded coconut
1 cup coconut oil – *melted*
¼ cup maple syrup
2 100g bars of dark chocolate

1. Melt the coconut oil on a low heat.
2. Mix in the shredded coconut and the maple syrup.
3. In a wax paper-lined tray, spread out the mix about 1cm/½" thick. Press down with a wet hand to pack it well.
4. Leave in the fridge to harden.
5. Cut the coconut into squares.
6. Melt the chocolate bars. Allow to stand a few minutes to cool.
7. Take each square and dip into the chocolate, covering it completely.
8. Lay out on clean wax paper, sprinkle with a little of the shredded coconut for decoration and return to the fridge to set.

Make lots because they will be very popular!

These blank pages have been inserted on purpose; for your comments, other recipes, ideas... use them!

These blank pages have been inserted on purpose; for your comments, other recipes, ideas... use them!

ESSENTIAL FARE

These foods will be the core of your cooking, sometimes all your cooking.

The recipes in the previous sections are combinations of these foods with small changes and added ingredients. Once you have mastered these you will be able to make an unlimited combination of dishes and meals.

RICE

BEANS & LENTILS

PASTA

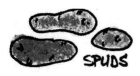

SPUDS

VEGGIES

BREAD

Potatoes

If I had to eat only one type of food it would be potatoes, especially if I could add a little fresh garlic, a nice drizzle of olive oil and a sprinkle of salt!

Potatoes are to a large extent starch, the energy part of our diets. If eaten whole, with the skins, they also have a lot of vitamins and minerals.

Some people are known to peel their potatoes, I do not. There are small, very small, minerals and important nutrients that hide in the skins of root vegetables and the only way to get them is to eat them. And I think potatoes taste better with their skins, the complete meal.

If you must peel them, it is better to do this after they are cooked (unless making mashed potatoes) as they may break apart and become mushy, losing much of their taste and nutrients in the water.

> *N.B. I have several pages of potatoes because they are so important, especially to me!*

Steam – Steaming means cooking with water but not in the water. Scrub the skins well, then put them in a few centimetres/1 inch of water. A metal holder can help keep them off the bottom. Bring the water to the boil, then simmer with the pot covered. Depending on the size of the potatoes, they may take from ½ hour to an hour to cook. Check after a time to see that all the water has not evaporated.

To check if they are cooked, use a knife to prod them; when the knife goes through easily, they are cooked.

Boil – Scrub the skins well. Put them in the pot and cover with water. Bring water to the boil then simmer until cooked. Cooking time will depend on the size of the potatoes, approx. 40 minutes for medium sized ones. To check if they are cooked, use a knife to prod them; when the knife goes through easily, they are cooked.

Do not cook on high heat as you will burst the skins and they will fall apart.

Mashed potatoes – If you prefer, you may peel the potatoes first and cube them, but I like to make mash with the skins on. Cubed or quartered, half cover with water, bring to the boil then simmer. They cook fast, approx. 10 minutes or less. I will often peel a clove of garlic and toss it in whole with the potatoes.

Drain the water from the potatoes but keep it. Add a little olive oil and a good pinch of salt. Mash them until there are no more lumps. If the mash seems too dry, add a little of the potato water and mash some more. Serve right away, piping hot.

Bake – Scrub the potatoes well. Coat them with a little oil and place them on a tray in a hot oven at 220°C/430°F. They should be cooked in less than an hour. Test them with a knife to see if they are cooked. The oil will give the potato a lovely chewy skin. Sprinkle with a little salt before serving.

I like to eat the skin of baked potatoes, not just the inner flesh, another reason to wash them well. Once cooked, split the potato in two and fill them with anything you like; baked beans, roast veggies, chilli – well, nearly anything, or just a drizzle of olive oil, a sprinkle of salt and even a little fresh crushed garlic. Wonderful!

Oven Chips – A recent craze of students is to make chips (French fries) in the oven. Much easier and less greasy than deep fried. Cut them to the desired size, soak in water for 10 to 15 minutes to remove some of the starch, drain the water, dry them with your tea towel. In a large bowl drizzle a little oil on top, mix well, then lay them out on your oven tray and put into a hot oven at 220°C/430°F. You may wish to turn them once or twice to crisp them all over. Ready in approx. 30 minutes.

Adding some garlic powder, smoked paprika and chilli powder gives them a new delicious flavour.

My niece Keelin, who was reviewing the book for me, reminded me that a good grind of fresh black pepper is essential!

Fried – Home Fried Spuds! This was my father's favourite late-night snack. Any leftovers were always welcome. We quickly learnt to make them ourselves.

Scrub the potatoes, slice them in thin rounds, put them into a frying pan and drizzle with plenty of oil. Get them sizzling then lower the heat to medium. Leave uncovered; this will help them get crispy. Turn them from time to time so they do not burn, and they cook evenly.

One trick to speed things up, which is important when hungry, is to blanche the sliced potatoes in boiling water for a minute or two, drain and dry with a tea towel then add them to hot oil in the pan. Another suggestion from Keelin – she must like the dear spud as much as I do! – when cooked, sprinkle with a good bit of sea salt… eat with lots of ketchup or nice Dijon mustard!

Pasta

Always have pasta and a jar of tomato sauce on your shelf. Often the sole diet of many a college student. An important fast food – cooks in 10 minutes or less, and cheap!

Pasta is flour and water, normally made with wheat flour, semolina, with high gluten content; this is what holds it all together. It comes in many different shapes – long and thin, wide, flat, short and curly.

Today there are many varieties of pasta made with corn, spelt, even vegetables.

Cooking pasta

Bring a large pot of water to the boil, add a pinch of salt, drop in the pasta and give it a good stir. That's it. Keep the heat up and do not cover.

Depending on the thickness, dried pasta can take from 7 to 12 minutes to cook. You will have to taste it after a few minutes to know when it is ready – take some out and bite it. You want it still a little firm, 'al dente' – Italian for 'firm to the teeth'. Don't let the pasta get soft, it will lose its texture and taste. Fresh pasta cooks in 1 to 3 minutes.

Strain the pasta through a colander, or by using the lid of the pot to hold back the pasta as you drain the water out. Retain some of the water for re-heating. Return the pasta to the pot with your sauce and heat all together. You may need to add a little of the reserved water if it seems a little dry. Serve it hot, right away!

Rice & Grains

Grains are also starches, the energy force of our food chain. In whole form they are a powerhouse of nutrients and they taste great.

The most common grains are corn, rice and wheat. They are processed into breads, cakes, cookies, pasta, cereals and tortillas. In whole form, rice is probably the most common of all.

Rice

When cooking rice I use 1 cup of rice to 2 cups of water for wholegrain brown and 1½ cups of water for white or basmati rice.

Rinse the rice to remove any dirt and some of the dusty starch. Put the rice into cold water and bring to the boil. Cover the pot, turn the heat down and simmer until cooked. It is good to check a few minutes before the recommended time to make sure it does not overcook, unless you want mushy rice! Once cooked, use a fork to fluff it all up.

Brown – Long grain – wholegrain, the complete food.
Cooks in 20 minutes. Ratio: 1 cup rice to 2 cups water.

Short grain, brown – Organic short grain brown rice is the best, it cooks to a wonderful nutty chewy texture. It is so good that often I eat it by itself. Cooks in 40 minutes. Ratio: 1 cup rice to 2 cups water.

White – Long grain. One of the most common rice types found in shops. Cooks in 20 minutes.

Basmati – An aromatic variety popular with Asian cooking. It cooks up light and fluffy. Commonly found white, but also available brown. Cooks in 10 to 12 minutes. Ratio: 1 cup rice to 1½ cups water.

Quinoa

Quinoa is a small round seed. It has a light texture, is full of nutrients and goes well with any saucy dish. An ancient grain from the Andes that has grown in popularity around the world due to its high nutritional value and, of course, great taste!

It can have a bitter taste due to the outer shell. Soaking for 10 to 15 minutes in cold water first will help get rid of the bitterness. Discard the water.

Cooking: 1½ cups of water to 1 cup of quinoa. Bring water, quinoa and a pinch of salt to the boil then simmer. Cooks in approx. 15 minutes.

Couscous

Couscous is not a grain but a small form of pasta – wheat semolina. But it acts and is eaten like a grain, so I included it here. It is precooked and dried. All 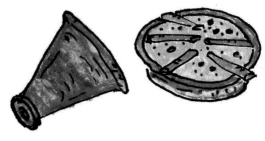 it needs is a minute to rehydrate, which makes it *very* useful. I always have some around, an ideal fast food.

All you have to do is pour boiling water over the couscous, give it a good stir and wait a minute. Add a little salt, perhaps a drop of olive oil and fluff it up with a fork. It is ready to accompany any rich saucy dish.

1½ cups of boiling water to 1 cup of couscous should do it.

Beans & Lentils

Beans and lentils make up the hearty part of a complete meal, the protein – the building blocks for the strong, healthy, beautiful body. Each region and culture, has its own special and unique varieties.

In the Middle East, the chickpea is the most popular bean and today its popularity has spread to other parts of the world, if only in the form of hummus. Haricot beans, which are in baked beans and tomato sauce, are popular in the British Isles and its older colonies. Black beans with rice are eaten in the Caribbean countries and kidney/pinto beans are used in much of Latin and South America for making the world famous chilli and refried beans. The soybean is used to make tofu, popular in much of Asia.

Beans

When starting to cook with beans I recommend using canned cooked beans. Even after mastering the cooking of beans, I still keep canned ones in stock; can't beat convenience and time.

Beans are dry, and some require soaking to rehydrate and help reduce cooking time. They can take from 1 to 3 hours to cook.

For the brave… home cooked!

Wash the beans well to remove dirt from the fields and from handling. For those that need soaking, 5 to 6 hours is recommended or, even better, overnight. Drain the soaking water and rinse the beans. In a heavy pot with a good lid cover the beans with plenty of water. Bring the water to boiling point then simmer until they are soft. Add salt only at the end otherwise it can make their skins tougher.

Beans – Cooking Times

Kidney beans – Red kidney-shaped bean, approx. 1½cm long.
Soak beans up to eight hours or overnight if possible.
Cooking time: 1½ hrs., maybe a bit more.

Pinto beans – Reddish-brown kidney-shaped bean, approx. 1½cm long.
Soak beans 6 to 8 hours before cooking.
Cooking time: 1 hr. or a little less.

Black beans – Black in colour as the name suggests!
Less than 1cm long.
Soak beans up to eight hours.
Cooking time: 2 hrs.

Chickpeas (garbanzo) – Roundish cream-coloured pea shape, approx. 1cm in diameter, sometimes smaller.
Soak chickpeas overnight.
Cooking time: 3 hrs+.

Lima beans – Flat kidney-shaped cream-coloured bean, approx. 2cm long.
Soak lima beans for an hour to allow them to hydrate.
Cooking time: 1 hr.

Navy/haricot beans – Cream-coloured bean, 1cm long.
Soak the beans up to eight hours before cooking.
Cooking time: 1½ hrs.

Lentils

Lentils are also important proteins. Unlike beans they do not require soaking, so they can be cooked right away. With lentils we can make stews, soup, even salads when cold.

There are several varieties but the three most popular varieties used in the recipes in the book are: brown, puy (green) lentils and red lentils.

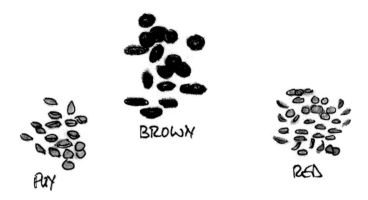

PUY   BROWN   RED

Brown lentils – Brown lentils have a strong, nutty flavour and are round and flat with a saucer shape, 5 to 7mm diameter.
Cooking time – 20 to 35 minutes depending on age of lentils.

Puy lentils – Puy (green) lentils are originally from France, are green and slightly smaller than brown lentils. They remain firmer when cooked, even a little chewy. They are used most often in stews.
Cooking time – 15 to 20 minutes.

Red lentils – Red and sometimes yellow lentils are most common in eastern dishes; they are actually split lentils and split peas. They are used in soups, or dahl – Indian stew.
Cooking time – 15 to 20 minutes, but can cook a little longer to soften well.

Vegetables

Vegetables can be eaten raw, made into salads or eaten alone as a snack – fresh food. You will often be cooking them as well, the key is not to overcook them. I repeat…

… the key is NOT to OVERCOOK them! Did you get that? Overcooked vegetables become mushy, lose their wonderful colour, their vitamins and, more importantly, their taste.

Aubergine (eggplant) – Aubergine has to be cooked. Some suggest salting aubergine first to take out the bitterness and reduce the moisture content. I do not always do it, but if you wish, sprinkle with a little salt, allow to sit for 30 minutes, then dry off with paper towel. Better to buy fresh ones, they are less bitter. To know if they are fresh, press them with your thumb – the skin should bounce back.

To fry, slice them into 1cm thick rounds and put them in a pan when the oil is hot (aubergine will soak up the oil if it is not hot enough).

You can also roast them in the oven, in rounds, cubed or halved. Bake at 180°C until the flesh is soft, then drizzle a little olive oil over them and toss well.

Broccoli – Break the head into florets of equal sizes. Put into a pot with 1cm of water. Bring to the boil and cover. Turn down the heat and simmer for a few minutes. The smaller the pieces, the quicker they cook. Broccoli cooks very fast, so keep an eye on it. To stir-fry, cut them up small – 1–2cm/1" or less in size – and cook in a pan on medium heat, with very little oil.

Cabbage – Steam or stir-fry. Chop it up in sizes you like, sprinkle with a little water, and cook in a covered pot on a gentle heat. To stir-fry, add a little oil to the pan and shake it up for a few minutes.

Carrots – Peel, then cut them into rounds, fingers or leave them whole. Boil or steam them, 5 to 15 minutes or so depending on their size. They are also very nice roasted in the oven or stir-fried with other veggies.

Cauliflower – Break the florets apart to desired sizes. Steam or boil the cauliflower for approx. 10 minutes.

Corn – Once the husk is removed, cook the cobs in boiling water for 10 minutes. They can also be cooked under the grill or on a BBQ, just keep turning them so they do not burn on one side. They will have a golden roasted colour when ready.

Courgette (zucchini) – I like to fry them in narrow lengths or in rounds. Courgette cooks quite easily. They can also be roasted in the oven and included in any stew. Wonderful cut into thin strips, grilled or roasted then coated in olive oil and garlic and sprinkled with a little salt.

Green beans – Steam or boil them in a little water, they only take a few minutes to cook. They can be stir-fried with a little oil and garlic.

Leeks – Wash them well as there is often sand inside the leaves. Chop them as small as you like and fry them gently in a little oil or in a little water. Used instead of onions they give dishes a different and wonderful flavour, great to give variety.

Parsnips – Boil or steam them like carrots. Oven roasted, they become sweeter, sprinkle with a little cumin and salt.

GREEN BEANS

Peas – Cook them in a little boiling water. Fresh peas or frozen will cook in a few minutes. When including them in other dishes they can be tossed in raw as they cook quickly.

Peppers – Peppers can be fried, cut into lengths, or oven roasted in large chunks, with a little olive oil and a clove of garlic. Actually, they are wonderful any way you cook them! Perfect stir-fried.

Roast peppers – Cut in half, remove the inner seeds, place skin side up on your oven tray and place under hot grill to blacken them fully. Remove the skin as they cool.

Spinach – After washing the spinach do not dry it, just put it into a pot and cook at a low heat. The spinach will quickly shrivel and wilt. Stir once or twice for it to cook evenly; this will only take a minute or two.

Turnip – Peel the harder outer skin, then cut into chunks. Boil or steam them. 10 to 15 minutes or so should be enough.

Bread

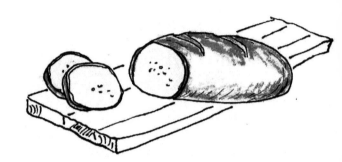

Most of us eat bread every day in one form or other. In some cultures, bread is a very important staple, in others an accompaniment to the meal and, of course, a prerequisite for the famous sandwich!

Bread can be made with yeast, which helps the bread to rise, making it light and giving you something to bite into. Bicarbonate of soda or bread soda is used in Irish soda bread instead of yeast. Some 'bread' is made only with flour, water and salt, such as Indian roti.

YEAST RISEN BREAD

The Dough

The dough will start to rise as the activated yeast creates air bubbles to make a light bread. This could take an hour.

3 cups strong flour (2 cups of white, 1 of brown gives it a wholemeal texture)

1 packet yeast, 7g perhaps (fast acting dry)

1 cup water – lukewarm

1 tsp salt

2 tbsp olive oil

1. Mix the yeast and water and allow it to sit for a minute or two. It should start to bubble a bit – the yeast is active.
2. Add this to the flour and olive oil. Mix well to combine and bring it together.
3. Knead it for about 10 minutes, which means pressing it down hard, folding it back, pressing again, over and over again. Your dough will become a little elastic and smooth. If it is too sticky, add a little flour. If it is too dry, add a little water.
4. Place the dough in your big bowl with a drizzle of olive oil so it does not stick to it. Cover with your tea towel or cling film and allow to double in size, approx. 1 hour.
5. Deflate the dough by punching it down, add the salt and knead it another minute to mix it in well. The dough is now ready.

Flat Bread – Pizza Base

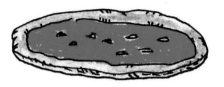

Once the dough has doubled in size, turn on the oven to 220°C/500°F.

Knead it again for 1 minute after adding the salt, then divide in two and roll it out with a rolling pin, or you can press out with your fingers until it is about ½cm/¼"thick. Place on your oven tray and let it 'relax' for 10 to 15 minutes until the oven has reached the correct temperature.

Cover with a layer of sauce and place in the bottom part of the oven for 5 minutes or until the bottom feels a little firm. Add the topping of choice then transfer to the top of the oven for another five minutes to crisp the toppings.

Bread Rolls

Using the same dough as for the flat bread, divide into 10 equal pieces. Make into round shapes, then place on a tray, cover with cling film or a tea towel and allow to double in size. This could take between 30 minutes and an hour.

Have your oven hot, 200°C/450°F. Place the tray in the middle of the oven for approx. 20 minutes. Tap the bottom of a roll, if it sounds hollow they are done. Allow to cool… if you can wait that long!

Pan Fried Naan

Make the dough, adding a teaspoon of sugar. Once it has risen, knock back. Take a small handful of dough and roll it out quite thin.

In a heated dry pan place the thin dough. After a minute or less it will rise or bubble. Look underneath to see if it has browned then turn it over for another few seconds to slightly brown the other side.

Take it off the pan and spread a little garlic infused veggie butter over it.

SODA RISEN BREAD

Corn Bread – Perfect with a hot bowl of chilli.

Making corn bread does not require any rising time. All that is required is to mix all the ingredients together and put it into the oven.

2 cups cornmea
1 cups wheat flour
1 tsp baking powder
1 tsp baking soda
1 tbsp nutritional yeast
I ½ tsp salt

2 tsp apple cider vinegar
¼ cup olive oil
1½ cups water

1. Mix the dry ingredients together in a large bowl.
2. In another bowl mix the water, oil and vinegar.
3. Pour the wet ingredients into the dry ones and make into a soft dough. You do not want it too dry and firm.
4. On an oiled tray spread out the dough to 2cm/1" thick.
5. Place on the middle rack of a hot oven at 200°C/400°F for approx. 30 minutes.

Check with a toothpick. If it comes out clean it is ready. Allow to cool before serving.

IRISH SODA BREAD

I was first introduced to soda bread by Peggy when I came to Ireland courting her daughter. It remains one of my favourite Irish foods and I still get to enjoy her brown bread today!

Makes one good loaf.

2 cups strong white flour
1 cup wholemeal brown flour
½ tsp salt
1 tsp bread soda *(bicarbonate of soda)*

1¼ cups soya milk or water
1 tbsp cider vinegar
1 tbsp olive oil

1. Mix together the flour, bread soda and the salt, then add the wet ingredients.
2. Make into a rounded cake about 3cm/1½" high. Cut a deep cross in the top, almost quartering it, and place onto the middle rack in the oven.
3. Cook for 15 minutes at 200°C then lower the oven temp. to 180°C and cook for another 30 minutes.

Check if it is cooked by tapping the underside of the bread. If it sounds hollow, it is ready.

Pastry

Making pastry was quite daunting for me at first. I was shown how to do it, but it came out hard, not flaky. It took a good few tries until I mastered it. I also realised that it does not matter if it is not so flaky, it still tastes good… homemade!

FOR SWEET THINGS: PIES AND TARTS

2½ cups of plain (pastry) flour
½ cup of cold vegetable margarine
1 tbsp of sugar
2 tbsp of vegetable oil
4 to 5 tablespoons of cold water

APPLE TART

1. Mix together the flour and sugar.
2. Cut the vegetable fat with a knife into the flour until quite small.
3. Add the oil and mix together using the knife – I then use my hands to rub the flour through until you have a crumbly texture.
4. Add just enough water to be able to bring it all together into a ball and refrigerate for 20 minutes before rolling out.

FOR ALL THINGS SALTY:
SAVOURY PIES, SPANAKOPITA

2 cups of plain flour
½ cup of flour
½ cup of vegetable margarine
2 tbsp vegetable oil
1 tbsp nutritional yeast
4 to 5 tbsp cold water
Pinch of salt

EMPANADAS

1. Mix together flour, salt and nutritional yeast.
2. Cut the margarine with a knife into the flour until quite small, then add the oil and mix together using the knife – I then use my hands to rub the flour through until you have a crumbly texture.
3. Add just enough water to be able to bring it all together into a ball and refrigerate for 20 minutes before rolling out.

Take it out of the fridge and divide the ball in two – one for the base and one for the cover. Roll out with a rolling pin or press each half into an oiled dinner plate or pie dish.

These blank pages have been inserted on purpose; for your comments, other recipes, ideas... use them!

Pancakes

... the thick ones!

Pancakes may not exactly seem like a staple food, but my cousin Dawn asked me to include them – why not part of a staple diet?

They can either be sweet or savoury. Plain with a little sugar or savoury with potato, fried onions and chives.

FAT FLUFFY PANCAKES

Makes enough for 10 medium pancakes.

For the savoury type – add ½ tsp of salt and mashed potatoes and herbs.

1½ cups of plain flour
2 tsp baking powder
1 cup of almond/soya milk
½ tsp sea salt
2 tbsp olive oil
2 tbsp sugar (omit if savoury)
Vegetable oil (grape seed) for frying

1. Mix everything together to make a smooth batter then allow it to stand for 10 minutes so all ingredients combine well.
2. Get your non-stick frying pan nice and hot. Drizzle a little oil into it and pour in a big spoon of batter. I can usually make three at a time in a large frying pan.
3. Wait for bubbles to appear on the surface.
4. Check the underside of the pancake; if it is browning flip it over until the other side is brown, perhaps another minute more.

My favourite topping: Canadian maple syrup, but stewed fruit is also very nice. I sometimes add a few blueberries or sliced bananas to the batter.

For savoury ones, eat with sour cream. Tahini sauce is good with plenty of garlic.

CRÊPES ... *thin pancakes*

Crêpes is the French name for pancakes. They are made very thin without any rising agent. Perfect rolled up with a filling and covered in a little sauce.

Thin French Crêpes – savoury
Makes approx. 10 large crêpes.

2 cups of plain flour
2 cups of almond milk
2 cups of water
1 tbsp olive oil
½ tsp sea salt

Vegetable oil (sunflower oil) for frying

For the sweet version: add 2 tsp of sugar and omit the salt.

1. Mix everything together to make a smooth runny batter. Allow the mixture to stand for 20 minutes in the fridge before using.

2. Get your non-stick frying pan hot and drizzle a little vegetable margarine or olive oil into it.
3. Spoon approx. 3 tablespoons of batter and quickly twirl around the pan to spread it as thin as possible.
4. Once brown on one side, flip over and brown the other. Stack them on a plate to cool until ready to use.

For the filling in savoury crêpes I like creamy mushroom sauce with wilted spinach, see p. 160. Fill, roll and warm in the oven at 180°C/350°F for 10 minutes before serving.

For Sweet ones, a squeeze of lemon juice and a dusting of sugar as they come off the pan. I also like a generous dousing of maple syrup.

MEALS

... what to cook?

At times the hardest part is figuring out what to make. I start by checking for leftovers and then build the meal around them, easier and quicker. Otherwise I check the cupboards and the vegetable drawer and try to come up with ideas.

Of course, the meal will vary depending on the occasion, how tired you are and on your hunger!

CHILI BEANS

BAKED PATATOES

COOKED CARROT

GREEN SALAD

A MEAL! COMPLETE

Appetite Teasers

*... To start, to taste,
or just to tease.*

You may be having a few friends over and you just want something to nibble on – food is a must for good conversation. Perhaps you are having a gathering and as your guests arrive you offer them a drink and an appetite teaser… buying time.

Bruschetta

You can never go wrong with **tomato, garlic & olive oil!!!** A little toasted bread and this lively mixture on top. This should only be made fresh (**p. 76**).

Hummus and veggies

Cut up carrots into sticks, broccoli tops into florets, red pepper into strips, even celery sticks, courgette, cauliflower florets, … reduced to bite size.
Crudité - Raw & Fresh
Serve on a platter with a bowl of hummus in the middle (**p. 78**).

Guacamole

If you have a big bag of corn chips and a bowl of guacamole everyone will be happy. Ripe avocado, a little lime juice and garlic. **(p. 79)**

Stuffed Mushrooms

This is the ultimate 'umami' dish. Savoury, strong flavours in a mouthful – and **people cannot stop eating them!** Make many of them, 4 or 5 for each person, each big enough for a bite or two. **(p. 130)**

Brunch

... Late breakfast, early lunch

I really like to eat breakfast late on weekends. Spend as long as possible in bed... hum ... and when really hungry, take the time to enjoy it.

The later in the morning the better – a bit of breakfast, a bit of lunch. The weekend newspaper, a few friends or your lover for company…

No Work – just put it all out!
Have a look in the fridge. Anything that can be eaten without much preparation. A few tomatoes, any spreads, hummus, olives, jams, cereal… leftovers can be easily heated up! Then just keep bringing on the toast and pots and pots of tea or coffee.

The **Big Fry** – if you are full of energy or you may just need the energy!

Cook up some home fried potatoes with onions, garlic & mushrooms **(p. 149)**.

Cut a few tomatoes in half and fry in your hot pan, veggie sausages from your freezer. A tin of those baked beans and plenty of toast.

The Decadent One – for that special occasion!

Here you actually have to plan it the day before.

Start with a nice bowl of fruit salad, made the night before **(p. 133)**. Next, pancakes with maple syrup, or stewed fruit **(p. 166)** / **(p. 136)**. Then spread out the olives, pâtés, savoury relishes and jams… with nice light crispy bread, Mediterranean butter beans **(p. 128)**.

… And plenty of good strong coffee.

If the morning has been quite late… with purpose, orange juice with a good portion of champagne sets you up to complete the wonderful lazy day!

Midnight Snack

... Home late and very hungry!

Home late? A good night out? A group of friends in tow and no one is ready to go home? Of course, ravenous. 15 minutes is all you will wait!

Pasta and Sauce

Boil up a big pot of water, throw in the pasta and open a jar of sauce – perfect to feed a group quickly.

No sauce? No worries – garlic, chilli flakes and a good splash of olive oil is all you need **(p. 150)**.

Home Fries

Nothing beats home fries! A bit of cutting, but worth it **(p. 149)**.

Chip Butty (Chips = French fries)

Eating 'chip butties' is an acquired taste… you acquire it after a long night out in the pub… A chip sandwich smothered in any sauce – garlic mayo is highly recommended **(p. 113).**

Introduced to us by Dr. Daithi, the connoisseur of such fine things. High fat, high cholesterol, but so worth it… Warning – not advised as regular sustenance.

Toast

Have you forgotten hot toast? Just cover it with interesting things:

Hummus, slices of tomato, black pepper and a drizzle of olive oil.
Garlic sliced super thin, and a chopped tomato. (Make sure your partner eats some as well!)
Mashed avocado, chilli flakes, and a little black pepper.

Of course, there is always peanut butter and jam!

Gang Of Lads

... Plenty of food and chat.

You are getting together with the 'lads', a gathering of really good friends, so you need drink, and plenty of food. One-pot meals are in order here – nothing fancy but hearty, tasty and filling.

Big Chilli

> *A NOTE: Before I get in trouble here, 'lads' is a unisex term used in some parts of the western hemisphere.*

Make the chilli the day before, so on the night you have very little to do. Chilli is always better the next day or the day after that **(p.95).**

You can serve it on toasted bread, with a bowl of rice or it is perfect as a filling for baked potatoes **(p. 147).**

Red Lentil Dhal

Everyone will have at least two bowls of it, so make enough!

The ginger and spices are addictive. (**p. 99**) Serve it with a warm pitta bread or on top of brown rice.

Chickpea Stew

This recipe enjoys slow cooking. Stewed garlic, red peppers and olive oil… wow! The chickpea is only the carrier (**p. 94**). Perfect with brown rice.

Minestrone Soup

Italian stew with everything in it – veggies, pasta, beans and lots of garlic, all swimming in a sloppy tomato broth (**p. 97**). Serve with big slices of crispy Italian bread.

PITA.

Table For Two

... Tête-à-tête.

This is not really about eating, is it? Yet food can put you in the right mood. Go light, you certainly do not want to overeat and fall asleep on the couch!

The first date... play it safe

- TOMATO SOUP – A small bowl and a hunk of bread (**p. 37**).
- ROAST VEGGIE SQUARES – Everyone likes puff pastry. A few roast veggies, the taste is 'sweet', as you want it (**p. 106**).
- Serve with baby potatoes and green leaf salad.
- APPLE CRUMBLE – Easy to make, and humble (**p. 134**).

Second date... some interest

- AVOCADO BRUSCHETTA – Serve two pieces each (**p. 77**).
- SPICY MUSHROOM PASTA – Tried and tested to win over hearts. Serve with good baguette and nothing else (**p. 63**).
- COCONUT SQUARES – They will be impressed (**p. 142**).

Back again... a serious affair

- LEAVES & BEANS SALAD – A hearty salad. If you are having lunch, this will suffice with a bit of bread (**p. 49**).
- TOFU BAKE – Serve with brown rice and French green beans (**p. 96**).
- SPONGE CAKE & STEWED FRUIT... there will be no going back! (**p. 137 & 136**).

Wait a few minutes before serving the next dish. Allow the first to settle and the appetite to grow... more time to be together, time to listen and time to admire!

The rest is up to you... I can do no more!

> *A NOTE: Do not give big portions, because you have several dishes; better to give small amounts or everyone will be full by the second plate!*

Group Of 6

... That small dinner party.

This is where I show off, and why not? I am the chef! Most of us who cook have big egos! Get the table set ahead of time, have the drinks at the ready, and a few appetite teasers, give them a taste of what's to come.

For the big meal I serve many dishes – different tastes, colours and choices. You may have a guest who doesn't like garlic, sacré bleu!

Mexican night

- CALABAZA SOUP – Something to warm the body. If you like it spicy, add ½ tsp of chilli flakes when cooking **(p. 38)**.
- AVOCADO & TOMATO BRUSCHETTA – Fresh and lively **(p. 77)**.
- BURRITOS – Serve with brown rice, a green leaf salad, fresh tomato salsa and tahini sauce. After this no one will be able to move **(p. 98)**.
- APPLE TART – Soya custard from the shop is perfect with it **(p. 135)**.

Veggie Supreme

- CAULIFLOWER CHOWDER – Sprinkle with chopped parsley for colour **(p. 35)**.
- LEAVES & BEANs SALAD – a good hearty salad, serve small portions **(p. 49)**.
- TOFU BAKE – Serve with mashed potatoes and curried spinach **(p. 96)**.
- SPONGE CAKE & STEWED FRUIT – Perfect on a cold night **(p. 137)**.

The Mediterranean

- TOMATO SOUP – Serve with herbs and garlic croutons **(p. 37)**.
- LINGUINE & PESTO – Sprinkle a few toasted pine nuts on each serving **(p. 65)**.
- PIZZA – Choose the toppings of your choice and serve rocket leaves or a green leaf salad. Make the pizza earlier or the day before and re-heat it… next day pizza tastes great! **(p. 82)**.
- CHOCOLATE-COVERED DATES – After that big meal you won't want anything else, maybe a nice strong coffee will suffice **(p. 141)**.

Let time pass between courses. Sit together and let the meal take effect, eat and talk. The laughter will soon fill the room – the real reason for the gathering!

Meet The Parents

... Time to impress.

Just being able to cook will be impressive enough!

Don't do anything too complicated. Just make sure it works, is something you have done before and that there is enough. Nothing worse than future in-laws going away hungry, it could be talked about for generations!

The snack

If they are only stopping for a drink, make sure you have food. Something small and warm is always impressive, and make it finger food.
- STUFFED MUSHROOMS (**p. 130**).
- BRUSCHETTA or (**p. 76**).
- Mini VEGGIE SQUARES – cut them into 3cm x 3cm sizes. (**p. 106**).

Lunch

Make this casual, like your own lunch. Serve the squares on the plates and have them serve themselves the rest.
- ROAST VEGGIE SQUARES and a few baby new potatoes from the oven, a cherry tomato sauce and a green leaf salad (**p. 106**).
- COFFEE with CHOCOLATE-COVERED DATES – (**p. 141**).

Full dinner

Set a nice table with a tablecloth and napkins and have the bottle of wine open and on the table. Start with any of the appetite teasers in the book and two other courses.

- GUACAMOLE and corn chips to start, just enough so they want more to eat, then sit them down (**p. 79**).
- TOMATO SOUP – It is light, perfect to start. They will like your homemade croutons (**p. 37**).
- LASAGNE – serve it with roast potatoes and crispy garlic bread. A little salad is always appreciated (**p. 100**).
- APPLE TART – Parents love apple tart (**p. 135**).

These blank pages have been inserted with purpose; for your comments, other recipes, ideas... use them!

APPENDIX

All the other stuff...

A table set is one of the most inviting and classy images. When all else is lost, class* must remain. If you do not have it, strive for it!

I have been cooking for a long time, yet I need from time to time to look up certain information – cooking times and temperatures, and a conversion table is invaluable in our era of globalised cooking!

> *A NOTE: *Class (Definition del Mundo) To comport oneself with dignity, generosity and kindness.*

Setting The Table

"Welcome to my table". To open your house and feed someone, to welcome anyone to your table, is a true act of generosity and kindness.

I set the table every meal. And if it is a special night I make it shine. When having people over, make sure the table is set before the meal is ready and especially before anyone arrives. It is an invitation as they walk in, it makes the occasion a celebration.

Basic Table

Plates
Knives and forks
Glasses
Bowls, if you are having soup, and spoons
Napkins (yes, use napkins, remember those hands)
A bread basket

The kitchen should be well lit. I don't go for dim lighting (unless it is for a tête-à-tête). The light is warm and welcoming, step right up. Plates, bowls if you are having soup or stew, forks, knives and spoons. To some, the positions of the cutlery has importance, to me no.

And napkins – one must wipe one's mouth, one's hands… and you will definitely need them if you are having spicy food, if only to wipe the sweat off your brow!

A Little More Finesse

You may be young, a poor college student, a striving artist, but that is no reason not to show a little class.

When the moment is important, when you want a real celebration, do a little extra, make the effort and those joining you will feel it right away.

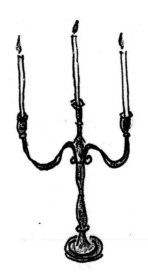

A tablecloth
Two plates – one for each course
Two glasses – water and wine
Candles

Cover the table with a cloth, not sure why but cloth just makes it. Those who share the moment with you will remember it.

Two plates when you are having a starter course. It looks great when you have two plates for these special dinners. A smaller one on top of the big one.

Candles, a minimum of two… candlelight just brings on a glow to the space, even during the day. And if you are really up for it, flowers – for a dinner table, better short ones otherwise they take too much space and you cannot see the person across from you!

Now let's fill those plates.

Serving It Up

How the food is presented will depend on the type of food you are serving, the occasion for the meal and sometimes the people you are feeding.

Self-Service

This is the easiest way to serve food. You put the various dishes on a counter, or leave them on the stove. Have plates or bowls at the ready and each person grabs one and fills it themselves.

This makes the serving job much easier, especially if you have a big group. People can take what they like, and get up when they want second helpings without the host (you) having to do much more. You can then enjoy the gathering as well. Purely relaxed.

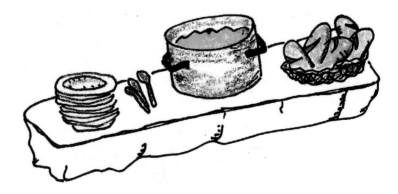

The Family Meal

The table looks good, colourful, inviting… All sit down, the serving dishes full of food are placed in the middle of the table or they are passed around and everyone serves themselves.

You can also serve up the main course, which might be too hot or too heavy to handle, like a big square of lasagne. The other side dishes, salads, etc. are on the table.

One takes as little or as much as desired. On the down side… if you are the last one in line, the dish may just be empty!!!

Full Service

My food, my creation, my way!!! Here the host, most likely the 'chef', makes up each person's plate.

When you do this, you are trying to create a combination of flavours, not too much of one thing, a little more of another… This method I prefer when I am making it an occasion.

And never load up the plates – put on less. If it is good, your guest will be asking for more, no better compliment!

My Dictionary Of Food

Today, many of us are familiar with a wide range of foods. Of course, there is always the internet when you have questions. But these are my definitions, from my limited knowledge and experience.

Aubergine (eggplant) – Purple-skinned oval-shaped vegetable, like a large egg (eggplant, naturally!) It can be eaten boiled, fried or baked, it goes with everything! Makes any dish special… **soul food.**

Avocado – Green savoury pear-shaped 'fruit'. They must be ripe, a light pressing of the thumb will tell you they are ready to eat – if they are not ripe, wait, do not eat. The main ingredient in guacamole… **soul food.**

When quite soft and you want to know if they are still good and not rotten, remove the small stem cap at the top. If green underneath, it is good. If dark brown… leave it behind.

Basil – Herb with a strong pungent taste when fresh, gives a great flavour to tomatoes. It can be mashed with a little olive oil, garlic and pine nuts to make pesto… **soul food**. A special sauce for pasta. I also like it over boiled potatoes.

Black beans – Small black kidney-shaped bean, less than 1cm long. Quite popular in South America and the Caribbean where the rice and black bean dish is a staple. Makes the best tasting bean burgers.

Butternut squash – also known as calabaza. Cream-coloured, smooth-skinned gourd, three times the size of a pear. The flesh when cooked can vary from yellow to orange. Perfect in soups, stewed or eaten with a little salt, a good grind of black pepper and a drizzle of olive oil.

Butter beans/lima beans – White flat kidney-shaped beans, come in different sizes. I like the large ones. Quite easy to cook. If you have time, cook them, the fresh cooked beans always have more flavour than the canned ones.

Calabaza – See Butternut Squash.

Chickpeas (garbanzo beans) – Pea-shaped, beige-coloured and very hard when dried and uncooked. They take a long time to cook, up to 3 hours, so the tinned version is very useful. Used to make a popular Middle Eastern paste called hummus… **soul food.**

Coriander (cilantro) – Green leafy herb, with a strong 'fresh' flavour and, I would say, addictive! A wonderful herb to have around. Perfect in curries, stews, with tomatoes – add it chopped, just before serving, it loses much of the flavour when cooked.

CILANTRO

Couscous – Pre-cooked type of pasta, with the texture of a grain. It only takes 1 minute in boiling water to finish the cooking. The ideal home-cooked fast food, always have some around. Add a little salt and, a little olive oil and it is ready as a bed for any saucy dish!

Cumin – Spice used in many eastern dishes. One of my most important spices, gives a full flavour to any dish. I like to use them whole added to onions while they are sizzling. Not only for curry dishes, but also for bean dishes, especially chilli.

CUMIN SEEDS

Garlic – A small white-beige, sometimes pink, bulb which breaks apart into cloves. It has a most wonderful flavour… **soul food.** Some have been known to find the taste unpleasant, which I simply cannot understand!

Better used fresh, in salads and with tomatoes, even on warm toast. Also used in sauces. One of nature's gems – once you get hooked, you will want to use it in nearly everything… so have lots of it around! Garlic is known to have important health-giving properties, important for brain power… perhaps why I need so much of it!

Garlic and indigestion: Some people find garlic hard on their stomachs. I once met a Frenchman making a salad with big chunks of garlic, but he was removing the centre stem. He explained that the centre can be hard to digest.

Ginger – Beige-coloured root. An acquired taste, but once you acquire it, no turning back! A requirement for stir-fries, marinades, stews, and especially dhal. Simply remove the thin outer skin and chop it up.

GINGER

Green beans – Long green pods, thin as a pencil. Also known as snap beans, they break with a snap (or French beans) because the French eat a lot of them! Lovely as a side dish, steamed or stir-fried.

GREEN BEANS

Haricot/navy beans – White small kidney-shaped bean, 1cm long. The bean used for the popular British 'baked bean' recipe and in minestrone.

HARICOT

Kidney beans – Kidney-shaped beans, (easy, no?), the width of your thumb long. Dark red colour, quite popular for chilli. Cooking is long, so I try and have several pre-cooked cans in the cupboard. Wonderful source of protein for all you gym lovers & body builders. I use kidney beans for the refried beans… **soul food.**

KIDNEY BEANS

Lentils – Saucer-like in shape, lentils come in different sizes and colours. They are pulses like beans and peas. They cook quite easily and are strong in flavour. Great for stews. When cold add a little vinaigrette and a little parsley and you have a very nice salad.

LENTILS

Lima beans – See butter beans.

Millet – An ancient seed (grain) that has seen a renewed popularity because of its nutrient-rich properties and light flavour. A perfect combination with any saucy dish and often used as part of a cold mixed salad.

Mustard – Yellow strong paste made from the mustard seed flour, a little salt and vinegar. Used in vinaigrette and with fried potatoes.

Olive oil, **extra virgin** – I use oil in much of my daily cooking. Oils that are extracted from their fruit by mechanical means (extra virgin), are of much higher quality. I use cold pressed if I can get it. There is nothing better than the taste of a good quality extra virgin olive oil… it makes all the difference!

Oregano – Herb from the Med that has more flavour when dried. Used in tomato sauce for pasta, on pizza and in stews.

Parsley – Green curly herb, wonderful when added to salads, cooked mushrooms and potato dishes. Chop it fine then sprinkle over anything. Use it fresh. I have read that a little fresh parsley in the mouth will help rid of garlic breath.

Passata – Tomato passata. Cooked tomatoes passed through a sieve to remove the skins and the seeds… pure pulp. Used for tomato sauces or soups.

Peppers – Capsicum (Some are sweet and some are hot). Peppers can come in many colours and shapes. In shops we find mainly green, yellow and red or some shades of these. The red ones are the sweetest. Perfect in

salads, in stir-fries, in stews, and wonderful oven roasted with a drizzle of olive oil and garlic (sorry!).

The hot/spicy varieties are often smaller and narrower, used for curry dishes and in chilli.

Pesto – A paste made from fresh basil, pine nuts and olive oil… **soul food.**

Portobello mushrooms – Large mushrooms about the size of your palm. They are cream-coloured on top and dark brown underneath.

Pinto beans – Kidney-shaped beans. They look like kidney beans but are milder tasting, light brown in colour and with a softer skin when cooked than kidney beans. They can be almost creamy in texture. I like using them in chilli or bean stews. They are easier to cook than kidney beans.

Puy lentils – Small light green/brown, very popular in the Mediterranean region. They make a wonderful stew with carrots and potatoes.

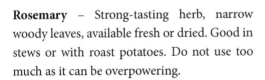

Rosemary – Strong-tasting herb, narrow woody leaves, available fresh or dried. Good in stews or with roast potatoes. Do not use too much as it can be overpowering.

Red lentils – Actually, red 'lentils' are split peas. Cooked they turn a golden yellow colour and they break apart to make a type of mash. They cook easily and are great for soups and stews. Used in Indian dahl.

Spring onions (scallions) – Long slender bulb of the onion family. The lower part is white and upper part green. Eaten with potatoes, salads, stir-fry... anything that needs onions.

SCALLIONS

Tahini – Paste/butter made from sesame seeds used to make hummus. A staple in the Middle East desert along with dates. Also a popular sauce for falafel. I even use it on burritos.

Tamari – Sauce made from soya beans. Tamari is from Japan. It is darker and has a stronger flavour than the more commonly found soy sauce.

Tofu – Soya bean curd. Available in block form, white and rather tasteless until marinated. If you freeze it, it changes texture, becoming chewy. Frying after marinating gives it flavour and a crispy texture. Used in stir-fry dishes.

TOFU

Vinegar, apple cider – Fermented wine or juice. I like to use a good apple cider vinegar. Balsamic vinegar has become popular; a sweeter Italian vinegar from grapes, it can be drizzled over salads. The white type is only a chemical and should only be used for cleaning!

Apple cider vinegar is very useful for minor burns in the kitchen. I just wrap the area with a towel soaked in cider vinegar and after 20 minutes the pain is gone.

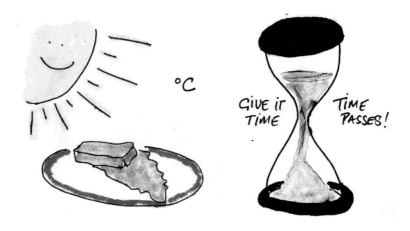

Times & Temperatures

Most of the recipes have cooking times and temperatures. You may need a quick look for easy reference.

	TEMP °C	TIME
Beans & Lentils		
Beans – Green …	Low	10–15 min
Beans – Lima/Pinto …	Simmer	60 min
Chickpeas …	Simmer	2 hrs+
Lentils …	Simmer	20 min
Dahl …	Simmer	20–30 min
Burritos …	180	20 min
Bread		
Pizza Thin …	220	10 min
Pizza Thick …	220	+ 5 min
Brown bread …	200	45 min
Bread rolls …	220	15–20 min

	TEMP °C	TIME
Pasta		
Pasta …	High	7–10 min
Lasagne …	180	30–40 min
Potatoes		
Potatoes – Baked …	200	45 min
Potatoes – Boiled …	Low	30–40 min
Potatoes – Fried …	Med	30 min
Potatoes – Roasted …	200	45 min–1 hour
Rice		
Rice – Brown …	Simmer	40 min
Rice – White …	Simmer	20 min
Veggies		
Veggies – Roasted …	180	20–30 min
Onions – Fried …	Med	5–10 min
Broccoli …	Simmer	5 min
Carrots …	Simmer	10 min
Dessert		
Tart, Pie – Apple …	180	30 min
Cake, Chocolate …	180	60 min
Peanut Butter Cookies …	180	10 min

Conversion Tables

Cookbooks may come from a different part of the globe. Temperature can be read in Fahrenheit or in Celsius. Recipe measurements can be in volumes or weights and appliances can use electricity or natural gas.

Temperatures

Celsius	Fahrenheit	Gas Mark
°C	°F	PG
110	225	¼
140	275	1
150	300	2
180	350	4
200	400	6
220	425	7
230	450	8
240	475	9

Weights

Grams

Grams | **Ounces**

Grams	Ounces
25	1
50	2
110	4
225	8
501	16 (1 pound)
1000 (1 kilo)	2 pounds + 4 oz

Volumes

Cups	Millilitres	Fl. Ounces
1	250	8
¾	190	6
½	125	4
¼	65	2
Tsp	5	teaspoon
Tbsp	10	tablespoon
Pinch	A two-finger grab	
A drop		1/2 a tsp

Knife Sharpening 101

The knife is the most important tool in your kitchen. Yet it is often the most neglected – it is simple to keep sharp and it will make your work so much easier.

- Sharpen every day before you start your main meal of the day. Of course, even I do not follow this rule... but when I try to cut a tomato and the knife won't go through it, I sharpen it. The result always feels great.

- If you have a sharpening stone, you are lucky, they are not very common these days. What are popular are sharpening steel 'swords' or honing steel. But I like the traditional stone.

- Wet it first then, with your knife almost flat but not quite, run the length of your blade back and forth on one side then on the other side of the knife. Do this maybe 10 times on each side then test if it is sharp. If not it needs a little more work.

If you do not have a sharpening stone, and you need to sharpen the knife, use a pottery mug. Turn it upside down, there is a rough unglazed rim, wet it and sharpen your knife with it. It should be enough to cook for that day.

Acknowledgements

This is not a solo effort...

The material which makes up this small repertoire of food has been acquired over time. Much of it learnt from my mother, ideas found in good cookbooks, inspirations borrowed from other chefs, common recipes modified to suit my tastes, and new ones created by choice or by accident.

To the many who have inspired me, **thank you**!

People mentioned in the book, more or less in order of appearance, who edited, commented, tested, influenced, supported and criticised when necessary:

Emma – for your help with editing, your many comments and challenges to my cooking and, perhaps most importantly, your push to "just do it"!
Carmel – for your patience with my culinary exploits and tolerance for my passion for garlic (even in bed!).
Maman – for being my first teacher and family chef. For pushing me towards a plant-based culinary lifestyle and for your tireless campaigning for the humane treatment of animals.
Fred – for showing me that salad and red wine is a perfect combination.
Teresa – for the marvellous meals I have enjoyed at your table.
Mary – for your kindness and culinary generosity.
Liam – for having the courage to take over my kitchen and teaching me something new.

Anne Marie – for your continuous support and your love of pasta.

Isabelle Brennan – for your continuous encouragements and appreciation of your father's culinary attempts.

Paddy – for your love of food and serious interest in veganism.

Maeve – for your editing and wonderful cooking every time I share your table.

Tommy – for your comments and improving the all-important refried bean – soul food.

Colm – for your brown bread, and for being the family's personal pizza chef.

Saeid – for giving me shelter and sharing your food all too often.

Sarah – for introducing many young Londoners to the wonders of vegetarian cuisine.

Dominique – for all your contributions, editing and advice, even the ones I had to ignore… "I think you use too much garlic!"

Sheila & Jim – for sharing your meals throughout the years and the wonderful inspiring cooking… and the love and laughter!

Neelam – for your warm welcome and having us to your table and sharing your tasty cooking.

Mairead – for your inspiration and ideas and most wonderful cooking.

Papa – for feeding me and teaching us the art of late-night cooking.

Permjit – for introducing us to the secrets of dahl cooking.

Muhammad – for teaching me how to make wonderful food from Syria.

Lily – for your patience in the kitchen and your recipe for veggie mayo.

Rory – for your positive comments that inspired me to write this volume.

Malachi & Evelyn – for your wisdom, kindness and feeding me.

Peggy – for your brown bread, apple tarts and much, much more.

Dawn – for teaching me that all sweet things come from heaven.

Casey – for showing me how to make the perfect Canadian peanut butter cookie.

Aveen – for your strong vegan convictions and wonderful sweet things.

Keelin – for your editing, seasoning advice and insights into the adolescent mind.

Daithi – for introducing us to the famous chip butty.

Brian – for your editing and suggestion that "I season the book with more of my personality"!

Edyta – for looking over the entire draft, finding errors and giving advice.

A very special thank you to **Kris** and **Frank** for their financial assistance with this project and their continuous encouragement and support.

The Index

For anyone wishing to contact me, for information or questions about the recipes or queries about cooking, please send me an email.

As well if anyone would like more information on veganism and plant-based diets – the positive affects on our health, how it affects the environment and the treatment of animals please send me an email.

thehungrysoulseries@gmail.com
@follow_hungrysoul

Jacques